THE WAYWARD PROFESSOR

The Wayward Professor

Joel J. Gold

Illustrations by Vivian S. Hixson

UNIVERSITY PRESS OF KANSAS

Published by the University Press of Kansas (Lawrence, Kansas 66045), which
was organized by the Kansas Board of Regents and is operated and funded by
Emporia State University, Fort Hays State University, Kansas State University,
Pittsburg State University, the University of Kansas, and Wichita State University

Library of Congress Cataloging-in-Publication Data

Gold, Joel J., 1931–

The wayward professor / Joel J. Gold : illustrations by Vivian S. Hixson.

p.   cm.

ISBN 0-7006-0404-9 (alk. paper)

1. Education (Higher)—Humor.   2. Universities and colleges—
Humor.   3. College teachers—Humor.   I. Title.

PN6231.C6058   1989

814'.54—dc19   89-5290

CIP

British Library Cataloguing in Publication Data is available.

Printed in the United States of America

10   9   8   7   6   5   4   3   2   1

The paper used in this publication meets the
minimum requirements of the American National
Standard for Permanence of Paper for Printed
Library Materials Z39.48-1984.

CONTENTS

Storytelling / 1

ACKNOWLEDGMENTS

Slightly different versions of the following tales originally appeared in periodicals: "The Paper Shredder" in *Ford Times*; "Kneecapped in the Art Museum" in *Report from the University of Kansas*; "Revenge of the Kanji" in *Winds: The Inflight Magazine of Japan Air Lines*; "Satire à la Sartre," "The Hazards of Humor" (in part), "The Two Cultures and Dr. Franklin's Fly," "Memoirs of a Library Collector" (in part), "Academic Conventions," "The Ph.D. and the IRS," "Ingenuity and the Grant Application," "Party Time in Academe" (in part), and "September Song" all in the *Chronicle of Higher Education*.

If this were an academic book, I would express my gratitude to all who helped with criticism, anecdote, or timely laughter: my editors at the *Chronicle*, Frances H. Oxholm, Beverly T. Watkins, Edward R. Weidlein; the staff at the University Press of Kansas; my non-wayward colleagues Sandy Cook, Stephen Goldman, Bud Hirsch, Michael L. Johnson, and James Gunn; two supportive word-processing whizzes, Sandee Kennedy and Pam LeRow; my wife, Ellen, and daughters, Jennifer, Alison, and Katy, sources and critics; and, of course, all the friends, American and English, who set me straight again and again.

But it isn't. Never mind.

STORYTELLING

I can remember very well the moment when I began to think about writing the stories which fill this volume. One or two of the pieces in it—the showdown on the streets of Wells, England, in 1762 and the one about Benjamin Franklin's drowned flies—had already appeared in print, but they were merely whimsical aberrations from more scholarly undertakings.

The moment of revelation was also a moment of extreme panic for me and one I should not like to go through again. I was reading a paper at a conference on eighteenth-century studies at C. W. Post College on Long Island. My topic was the radical politics of John Glynn, a serjeant-at-law, defender of left-wing causes in the England of George III. I had laid out the talk, as I usually do, to interest the audience—some facts about the man, followed by an account of events, sprinkled with courtroom dialogue from contemporary magazines and newspapers, and a verbatim account of a specific trial. I wanted to show Glynn in action.

Because of the eclectic nature of the conference I was sandwiched between a wide-ranging discussion of radicalism in France at the time of the Revolution and a detailed, close analysis of the Dutch Republic during the Seven Years War. I was greatly impressed by the two learned scholars who presented staggering amounts of significant evidence and many intriguing conjectures about the state of radicalism in the Netherlands and France during the middle and later eighteenth century. As a matter of fact, their papers relieved me of one of the constant worries at such conferences—that some erudite or crusty specialist in the audience will raise all sorts of difficult questions about which you know little. I decided that whatever questions might arise would be for the French historian or the Dutch political scientist. I relaxed.

For a time the assumption seemed well founded. The two of

them handled their questions deftly, and I smiled benignly at them and their interrogators.

Then it happened. A man in the third row stood up and announced: "The papers on the French Revolution and on the Dutch Republic were excellent, but I have something to say to Professor Gold." I tried very hard to look ready, knowing, competent. The expression I did achieve could probably be best described as terminal anxiety.

"You know what you are?" he asked, pausing dramatically.

The interval could not have lasted more than two or three seconds, but in that snippet of time my academic career flashed in front of my glazed eyes before it went up in smoke. It's been a good ride, I thought. They never caught on to how little I knew when they gave me a Ph.D. My first teaching job was a fluke. I had been promoted and tenured in the go-go sixties when everybody who could read and write was promoted and tenured. And now to be found out at this obscure conference after all this time. My only consolation was that we were there at little C. W. Post buried in a wooded estate in the middle of Long Island. It might take months, possibly a year, before news of my disgrace filtered back to the dean and my colleagues in Kansas.

His dramatic pause concluded, my assassin went on. "You," he said, "are a storyteller."

I was still functioning in the fear and destruction mode and consequently heard "storyteller" as a variant of "liar."

But he jarred me again when he then complimented me on the way I had laid out and presented the material on John Glynn. He had thoroughly enjoyed it! I could not respond to him at all when he finished. The blindfold had been too suddenly removed, the cigarette snatched too recently from my lips, the last-second reprieve read out too casually to the disappointed firing squad. But the next day at lunch I worked my way over to the perceptive gentleman and thanked him for his judicious comments without mentioning what I had assumed he was going to say.

Later when I thought about being a "storyteller," my reaction was fairly negative: if it did not mean "liar" or even maker of fictions, it certainly had less than scholarly connotations. If people were to ask about me, as the heroine of *Pride and Prejudice* asks about the foolish Mr. Collins, "Can he be a sensible man?"—the answer would have to be, "No, he's a storyteller."

But gradually I grew to be more comfortable with the label and began to consider some of the stories I was in the habit of telling on myself among friends. They all seemed to fit rather well into Thurber's definition of humor as chaos recollected in tranquillity.

And so, occasionally adding a fictional fillip or two, I started writing down the near disasters and chaos of my academic career—from the research grants committees to the IRS audits, from the paper shredder to my Italian fiasco. My professional friends were intrigued but unimpressed. An editor of *Harper's* was amused but pointed out that Russell Baker had rather "preempted" the territory. When I brought this unfair advantage to Mr. Baker's attention, he suggested that if *he* were an English professor, he would "be content to count my blessings, as well as the caesuras in *King Lear*, keep a firm grip on my tenure, and take plenty of sabbatical years." Finishing the caesuras in *Lear*, I thought about following his advice, but when it came down to going on with the caesuras in *Coriolanus* or telling more stories, I hardly paused—too many caesuras already—and continued to reflect—tranquilly—on the chaos of my academic life. The results fill the pages of this book.

I did spend some time considering appropriate titles and had just about settled on *The Wayward Professor of English*. One afternoon I tried it out on a couple of colleagues. They appeared puzzled.

"I didn't know you held an endowed chair," one of them said.

"No," I answered. "I am unendowed."

The knowing glance they exchanged convinced me that shorter titles are best.

THE CLASSROOM AND ITS PITFALLS

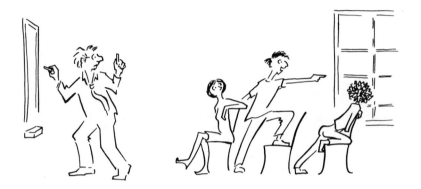

THE PAPER SHREDDER

Toward the bottom of the large pseudo-wood door of my faculty office there is a small hand-lettered sign that reads:

PAPER
SHREDDER

An arrow points to the space under the door where students are always sliding things—like late papers or requests for letters of reference. My colleagues see the sign and make little jokes, but most of them don't really know the story of the Paper Shredder.

It began simply enough a few years back when I was informing a class about the deadline for a set of critical essays. Allowing myself to be jollied away from the usual deadline of class time Thursday, I told them that papers could be submitted by 5 P.M. Friday. But no later. At 5 o'clock I would leave and turn on the paper shredder so that anything slipped under the door after 5 would be automatically shredded. Now it should be obvious in these straitened times that no garden variety English professor is going to have a paper shredder at his disposal. They all grinned back at me, and I figured we understood each other.

By 4:50 on Friday all but three essays had been turned in. In a few minutes I heard someone running down the hall, and a young man thrust his paper at me. "Plenty of time," I said. He looked almost disappointed that he was not the last. At 4:57 the next-to-last paper arrived. "Am I the last one?" the young woman wanted to know. Again disappointment.

It was 5 o'clock, and there was still one paper out. It was possible that it would not arrive, but the student was one of my conscientious overachievers. She was probably triple-checking her footnotes. I decided to wait. But there *was* all that talk about the paper shredder. I shut my door. I turned out my light. Then I pulled a chair up behind the closed door, gathered a couple of sheets of old ditto paper in my hand, and sat down to wait. I suppose I could have spent the weekend lurking in that darkened office. Well, I *hope* I would have been smart enough to leave by Saturday afternoon.

Anyway—and fortunately—at seven minutes past five I heard somebody running down the hallway toward my office. This was it—it had to be. Whoever it was stopped outside my office. And panted for a few seconds. As the paper began to come in under the door, I was ready.

With exactly the degree of pull that you get when you try to make change for a dollar in one of those airport bill-changing machines, I tugged slightly and evenly at the proffered paper. There was a slight moment of paralysis as the person on the other side of the door gripped the paper more tightly. Then, probably surprised at herself, she let go. I had her paper. I took the ditto sheets I had been holding all this time and began as noisily as I could to tear it into bits and pieces. Carried away by the dead silence on the other side of the door, I began to say aloud, "Chomp, Chomp, CHOMP." There was an audible gasp.

"Please, plee-ease," she said, "It's only seven minutes late."

I guess it was envisioning the scene outside my door that got me to giggling. (I know, I know. It was unworthy of me.) But here was this stricken young woman talking to the door. "Please, door, it's only seven minutes late." Perhaps the muffled giggling or the implications of the "Chomp, Chomp, CHOMP" had just registered, but I heard the closest thing to a "Humph!" I have ever heard in real life before she stalked off down the hall. I suppressed my giggles, collected my papers and my composure, and went home.

She wasn't in class the next period (I don't think she held a grudge, but she never trusted me after that), and I told the story— without names, of course. The class loved it. "Chomp, Chomp, CHOMP!" they kept repeating throughout the hour.

I repeated the story the following semester and the one after that—you can get a lot of mileage out of a good story. Students began to ask me about the paper shredder, and that's when I decided on the sign for the bottom of the door. And for a couple of semesters it was Our Joke. But you know how it is—sooner or later the old retired gunslinger is going to have to draw one more time. One of my honors students actually had the nerve to say, "You're always telling us about what you did to other classes, but you don't ever *do* anything like that." Now it was my turn for a "Humph!"

So amid the groaning about the deadlines for papers in The Comic Spirit course was born the idea for One More Twist. Essays were due Friday by 5. "And then the paper shredder," they chortled. "And then the paper shredder," I agreed.

When 5 P.M. arrived, and six papers were still missing, I gathered up what I had, turned out the lights, and went home. That weekend I spent much of my spare time tearing pieces of paper into tiny bits and dropping them into a brown paper shopping sack. On Monday I even used the department's aging paper cutter to slice waste paper into strips before I tore them by hand and stuffed them into my sack. The secretaries watched in disbelief and some trepidation lest they, in these difficult times, be accused of wasting supplies.

At the proper time, I secreted my nearly full shopping sack inside a large book bag and went upstairs to the classroom. I surreptitiously pulled it out and hid it in my reading stand, planning to discourse on their essays at the end of the period.

It worked out even better. Halfway through the period, as I was shifting from *Northanger Abbey* to *Alice in Wonderland*, one of my anxious worrywarts raised his hand. "When," he wanted to know, "will you be giving back the papers we turned in last week?"

"I'm glad you asked me that," I said, quite sincerely. The students were now all sitting up waiting for the answer, not paying much attention to my hands which were reaching in behind the reading stand to move the sack into position.

"Those of you who turned your essays in by 5 o'clock last Friday will get them back at the end of next week." A slight groan: they had hoped it would be sooner. They always do. "For those who didn't meet the deadline, those who slid them under my door some time after 5 P.M.—and I'm afraid I don't know how many of you there actually were . . ."

By this time I was milking it, and they were hanging on every word. The sack was in the ready position.

"Those of you who turned your papers in late, should [I had lifted the sack high above the desk] come up after class [I was turning it upside down and thousands—thousands—of little shreds of paper were fluttering down all over the reading stand, the desk, the floor] and identify your paper. If you can."

There was an explosion of laughter, footstamping, pandemonium as the shower of confetti continued for about five seconds. They could not believe any university professor—tenured yet—would do anything so idiotic.

"Now," I went on in my best professorial rhythms, "let us consider the scene in which Alice finds the caterpillar sitting on a mushroom."

At the end of the period, while I was trying to gather up all the tiny bits of shredded paper and deposit them in the waste basket (the maintenance people already think the faculty has been eating too many mushrooms), I saw a few of my students in the doorway pointing at the debris, apparently explaining to friends and passersby what had just happened in this classroom. And I don't think they were discussing the Mad Hatter or the March Hare. At least not directly. The passersby shook their heads and whistled softly.

I know that somewhere down the road the old gunslinger will have to draw one last time, but I reckon I'm safe for a couple more semesters.

KNEECAPPED IN THE ART MUSEUM

S ometimes the greatest teaching opportunities happen spontaneously. Not everything can be plotted out in advance.

I remember one day toward the end of a course in the eighteenth-century novel, a young woman in the back of the room commented on the novels we had been reading—*Tom Jones*, *Tristram Shandy*, *The Vicar of Wakefield*—and how much she had enjoyed them. "But," she said, pointing at the small paperback I was holding, "*The Man of Feeling* is absolutely awful. It's just plain boring." I looked at the book in my hand. "You know," I said, "I agree with you," and with that I flung *The Man of Feeling* across the room where he hit the wall with a satisfying "thwack." The class burst into spontaneous applause. I have since then thought of that moment with some chagrin. Twenty years from now will they recall the marvelous scene in which Mrs. Waters turns "the royal battery"—she is bare-chested—on Tom Jones? Or the Widow Wadman's assault on my Uncle Toby in his sentry box? No. They'll reminisce about the day some professor—which one was he?—threw that book—what novel *was* that?—up against the wall. But I have to admit—it was *very* satisfying.

One of those golden spontaneous moments came up for me a few winters ago while I was teaching an honors proseminar in Satire. I had fourteen very bright junior and senior English honors students, and I was pleased to be able to link the written satire we were studying to a current exhibit at the Spencer Museum of Art— "Artists Look at Art." Among the forty drawings, paintings, sculptures, and so forth were a number of wry comic or satirical pieces. My first assignment for these students was an essay on the three "most satirical" works in the exhibit. It was a very subjective paper, of course, but it made them go to the museum individually, look, and reflect. Then, after I had read all their papers, I planned to meet the entire class over there and walk around with them as they explained their choices and their reasoning. All carefully planned.

As Laurence Sterne would say, it fell out differently. Or rather, I did.

The ice and snow of January were behind us, but February in Kansas is no slouch. Having slipped on the ice the previous winter, I was extra cautious as I picked my way around patches of ice and over piles of snow before I could get safely indoors at the art museum. When I hung up my coat and removed my boots, I still had five minutes before my class would arrive. I had told them to meet me in the lobby at one o'clock. I started across the marble floor of the lobby toward a bench.

I slipped on a dab of water left over from somebody else's boots.

And I landed on the same kneecap I had landed on the winter before. *Then* it had been outside. My wife and I had been headed toward our car, and I slipped, went down to one knee on the cement sidewalk, uttered a few mild profanities, and got up again. I hobbled to the car, drove us home, walked up the steps to the house, went in to make myself a stiff—a very stiff—martini, before sitting down with the evening paper. My knee hurt. Bad. I read the paper, flexing my knee all the while. *It* was getting a bit stiff. I went in to have dinner. Afterwards I dragged myself upstairs and crawled into bed. The knee had swollen to the size of a medium cantaloupe and felt worse than I imagine any cantaloupe ever felt. Although bending it was agony, I thought it would be better to keep flexing it in order to keep it from getting stiff. Through a mostly sleepless night I kept flexing. Macho-man was not going to be done in by any puffed-up patella.

By morning I could not stand. The doctor's office thought that, yes, an x-ray might be appropriate. After a brief sled ride to the car, I was driven to the doctor's office where x-ray photographs were taken. The doctor was reading them when he came in.

"Well," he said, "you've fractured the kneecap."

I was really quite startled. I had not been thinking in those terms: a man with a fractured kneecap does not go home and make himself a martini. Apparently, he does. If he's an idiot. But worse was to come. "The one thing I don't want you to do," the doctor was saying, "is to bend your knee. Very dangerous—could cause serious problems."

I let him see that I was properly impressed by this cautionary warning but did not think it was necessary to tell him how I had spent my night. He was a busy man.

The point of this long digression is to explain how I *knew* what had happened when knee met marble floor. I crawled to a bench, pulled up my trouser leg and observed the impressive purple eggplant which seemed to have replaced the knee. I did not flex it. Staff members were hovering over me, offering water, cold compresses, a call to a doctor. I accepted everything and upped the ante from Doctor to Ambulance. They phoned for one.

Meanwhile students were beginning to arrive for the class. They stood around me goggling at the eggplant and my occasional grimaces. It was one o'clock.

"We are met here today," I began. (I suspect that I didn't really sound that much like Abraham Lincoln at Gettysburg, but I was getting a bit sepulchral from the pain.) "I asked you to meet me here at the museum," I probably said, "so that we could walk around together and look at the works of art you wrote about." They were tremendously solemn now, glancing from the eggplant to each other. "I am not," I went on, "going to be able to stroll around the museum with you." They were nodding now. "But," I said—and the sound of a siren nearing the front entrance lent some urgency to my lecture, "I want you to walk about as *if* I were right there with you." Their rapt faces suggested that I could have sent them off into a minefield at this moment. The art museum staff looked impressed too.

Ambulance attendants were wheeling a stretcher in, and the students parted to make room.

"Pay special attention," I groaned as I was lifted to the stretcher, "to the Larry Rivers' 'Dutch Masters' painting and [Groan] the Dali, and the Venus looking at a television set. I . . ."

I was being wheeled out the door. I turned for one last look at my class. "Go," I said. "Win one for the Gipper." They turned reluctantly toward the exhibits. "Go!"

I have often wished that instead of the museum staff, helpful and sympathetic as they were, I could have had as observers half a dozen of our flintiest Kansas legislators, the ones who are always muttering how professors don't really teach, or how they always ignore undergraduates. I think I could have turned the appropriations budget around single-handed. Make that single-legged. It was my finest moment in teaching.

My class apparently spent the entire period walking around the exhibition and told me later how valuable the session was. But the last word belonged to one of the museum curators who wrote to me in the hospital: "Many men have been awed by art, but I don't know of any who have gone down to their knees."

It seemed a fitting epitaph.

THE BEAST IN THE CHAMPAIGN JUNGLE

The next best thing to getting a sabbatical year to do your own research is going to another campus for a semester or a year to be a visiting professor. Unburdened by committee meetings, student advising, examinations for graduate students, or the other clutter of any professor's life, the visitor teaches a few classes, puddles away at his or her research, and gets invited to lots of dinner parties. It is a good life, that of honored stranger.

Having played the game once at Bowling Green in Ohio, I was eager to try it again when my wife decided to go back to graduate school to work for a Ph.D. We were in London at the time, enjoying my first sabbatical, but we agreed that I would write to whichever universities admitted her to their degree programs. I would explain our situation and offer my services as a visiting eighteenth-century specialist.

Although I wrote to half a dozen schools, it was the University of Illinois which showed almost indecent haste in responding. Evidently my inquiry had reached the English Department head just as he realized that three of his eighteenth-century people had been granted leave for the coming year. He wrote a decidedly warm letter confident that we could work something out. Would I be kind enough to indicate, he added, the salary I expected to receive from my university for the coming academic year?

Unfortunately, Kansas was paying a great deal less than Illinois. I pondered the phrasing: "the salary I *expected* to receive." A man could *expect* almost anything, couldn't he? After considerable soul-searching (to be honest, I was afraid he'd telephone my chairman at Kansas and get the dollar amount himself), I gave him a reasonable, if slightly padded, estimate of $14,000. I was at his mercy, and I knew what that meant in the cut-throat world of academia: he'd offer me a thousand less, and I'd say, "Thank you very much." The letter which arrived in London the following week floored me: "Would a salary of $15,000 be agreeable?" Agreeable? It would be astonishing. I wrote back by the afternoon post to express my considered judgment that, yes, the salary he had mentioned would be agreeable. That evening the new graduate student and I skipped Ned's Fish and Chips at the top of our road and toddled down to the Strand for the roast beef and Yorkshire pudding at Simpson's. Very agreeable, that.

One of the satisfying extra benefits of the year in Champaign-Urbana was the credit I gained with our feminist friends. "It's refreshing," they said, "to see a man who is willing to make sacrifices, leaving his job for a temporary one so his wife can get a degree." It took me a little while to acquire just the right smile—benevolence mixed with quiet nobility—and a modest expression of denial with which to respond. It hardly seemed worthwhile to explain that I was not being bored to death on any committees, had no students to advise, and was earning at least a thousand dollars *more* than I would be if I had not sacrificed myself. So I stood around at parties, glowing with modest nobility, while I was being held up for less sensitive male chauvinists as a model of gentle manhood. A number of my former male friends became, as the English might say, courteous but not cordial.

In truth, the first semester started out uneasily for me. During my sabbatical year the news of home had focused on campus unrest, the marches, the sit-ins, and the violence. My own university had been featured in the international edition of *Time* under the heading of "Bleeding Kansas": the student union had burned and there had been casualties from gunfire. Clashes between protesters and police seemed, at least to those of us thousands of miles away, to be daily events on campuses across America.

Preparing to leave swinging London—Carnaby Street and micro-miniskirts in those days—I did what any sensible returning American professor would have done: I went down to Bloomsbury and walked into James Smith & Sons (Sticks & Umbrellas) Ltd. "Let me see your largest Irish blackthorn," I said to the elderly clerk. He brought out one which Dr. Johnson would have been proud to use against any ruffian or blackguard foolish enough to

present himself. Thus suitably armed, I accompanied my wife to the University of Illinois.

The first sights were not reassuring. All the locals wanted to point out the hot spots of the previous spring's battles between the students and the police. "Here's where the fighting started," they said, standing at the main intersection of town and gown. Nor was I soothed by the appearance of the Administration Building, cheek-by-jowl with the English Building where I was scheduled to work. Bullet holes pockmarked the brick walls. (Only recently a taxi driver had shown me the bullet holes in the Dublin post office, and I *knew* bullet holes.) The windows, obviously shattered, were covered by plywood decorated in multi-colored primitive art— raised fists and "Power to the People" slogans. Afternoon tea at the British Museum was a world away.

Entering a classroom for the first time in more than a year, I tightened my grip on the blackthorn and surveyed the incipient mob. I had determined that when the inevitable happened, when they came over the barricades (read "lectern") for me, I would swing my cudgel with all the force I could muster and take as many young yahoos with me as I could.

Nor was my preparation merely physical. In standard academic fashion I was Keeping a Journal of my portentous and clearly limited days at the University of Illinois. When the uprising flamed up, there would be a proper literary account of all the significant events—large and small—which had foretold it. With a certain degree of pleasure, muted, of course, by my awareness that I would necessarily have perished, I envisioned a sifter through the rubble coming across the charred but otherwise legible pages.

This reader who came too late might have found the early passages pregnant with implication:

Kept the blackthorn prominently on the desk between us as I checked attendance in Advanced Literature. Don't much like the looks of Mr. Gordon in the back row.

Gordon and Miss Kline do not think Keats is relevant. Neither do I, but there's something sinister about their *saying* so.

The sophomore survey class wanted to know why they had to finish *King Lear* by Friday. Some quick movements in the second row. Brandished my stick and distributed weight evenly on both feet. (I have been reading up on Self-Defense.) False alarm: my brightest student had dropped her notebook, and everyone else was trying to pick it up for her. Set the blackthorn down quietly.

Mr. Gordon announced publicly that Dylan was a better poet than all of the Romantics put together. He demanded that we read Dylan. I was surprised he even knew Dylan (a bit familiar, I thought, but, still, encouraging) and said that we would get to the moderns next semester. Declaimed a bit of "Do not go gentle into that good night" from memory just to show I was "with it." "Hey, man," young Gordon said, "Don't you know 'The times they are a'changin'?" I took this as a direct threat and pushed the lectern between us.

This kind of fraught commentary went on throughout September and half of October. Rereading the entries one crisp evening, I was pleased by the authentic air of foreboding I had caught, a nice flavor of imminent violence. Then I counted the entries. There were forty-three of them, a rather embarrassing number. And that was the first time it dawned on me that I might be living out the fable of Henry James's story, "The Beast in the Jungle," in which the protagonist *knows* his fate will be unique. Waiting for his singular destiny, he avoids marriage, close friendship, adventure, until one day he suddenly realizes that he has become the only man who has ever lived a life in which absolutely *nothing* happened.

I read my journal one more time. I stopped making entries. On some days I even neglected to carry the blackthorn.

There was to be one more turn of the screw. Mr. Gordon dropped by my office to request a letter of recommendation for graduate school. "You really turned me on to literature," he said. "The way you waved that big stick around to make your points. Far out!"

He is currently teaching at a small college in Ohio. Jane Austen, I believe.

FEAR AND TREMBLING
IN THE ENGLISH NOVEL

Activist students, progressive deans, and education theorists are always calling for "innovative teaching." Quaint and respectable Mr. Chips, who has been deciphering coffee stains on his old lecture notes and offering generations of students the eternal verities, now finds himself under pressure to be exciting and to stimulate his students. Even plodding professors of humanities are experimenting in the classroom.

I admit that it pained me to discard those valuable notes I had accumulated over the years, but, planning a new graduate course in The English Novel, I decided to take the plunge and try something never attempted before. Why should the scientists have a monopoly on the experimental method? I had gathered some hefty novels with interesting storytellers—*Tom Jones*, *Tristram Shandy*, *Bleak House*, among others—to demonstrate how readers respond differently to different narrators. I would subtitle the course Readers and Narrators. Why not, I thought, as the enthusiastic fit came over me, show them how a narrator could manipulate them? And so I began to plot against the poor unsuspecting students who had signed up for English 790.

A teacher is a kind of narrator, isn't he? And students are a bit like readers as they try to figure out what the class is all about. I know my colleagues in the sciences would not have been charitable about calling those assumptions hypotheses, but I was delighted to do so. Yellowed notes be damned. I would be an innovator.

When I think of those earnest graduate students struggling to compile enough coursework to earn a master's degree or a doctorate, I am a little embarrassed at what I did. But then science is a cruel master. My enrollment rosters appeared a day before I was to meet the class for the first time, and I noticed among the ten who had signed up a former student who was currently working for me as a research assistant. Her presence could destroy the experiment. She would immediately see through my act. But I decided to chance exposure. Fleming might have blanched when his bread grew moldy, but he went on. Pavlov might have grown somewhat queasy when all those dogs began to slobber, but he went on. Ignoring my former student, I would carry on.

When the curtain rose on opening day, I strode into the classroom, registered (without seeming to look) the fact that there were ten students all sitting in the front row. (Undergraduates would have spread over the room, but graduate students are an orderly lot and like to be up front where they will not miss any words while taking notes.) I sat in the chair behind the desk and did not look up at them any time in the next twenty minutes. I think this mole-like behavior worried them—it certainly would have unnerved me—but I couldn't see their reactions. (I learned later that some professors are too terrified of students *ever* to look at them, so perhaps my students took no notice of what appeared to them to be normal behavior for a college professor.)

I announced the course name—The English Novel: Readers and Narrators—the course number, my name, my office number, my telephone number, my office hours. I peeked. They were writing everything in their notebooks. Then I proceeded to read in a dull monotone the list of books for the course, the Library Reserve book list, the number of papers required and the dates they were due. I still had not so much as glanced at them. I announced that I would read the roll, and they were to respond if they were present. I did and they did. They must have wondered how I would ever know who was who since even during this process I did not look at them.

With these details out of the way, I described—in the same monotone—the course and its aims. I told them about how Narrators affect Readers, how Readers respond to a serious Narrator in one way, to a comic Narrator in another, . . . Then I read them two paragraphs from a book newly translated from the German. (It was quite a dreadful passage in English *or* in German.) And I read it in a staccato voice as if it had never been translated. I was aware from the scratching sounds that they were still taking notes frantically. I stopped reading.

"Take out a sheet of paper," I said.

Anyone who has ever been a student at any level will recall the fear and trembling such an announcement triggers. A piece of paper? Oh, my God, a quiz! The first day? How did I ever get into this course? How do I go about getting out of it? You remember. They all dutifully extracted a sheet of paper from their neatly ordered looseleaf notebooks. Their pens were at the ready.

"All right," I said, still seated at the desk, still ignoring what I knew must be a quivering mass of humanity now hanging on my next words. "You need not put your name on the paper." Waves of relief flooded across the front row. "Based on the first twenty minutes of this class, I want you to write down your expectations for it. What will the course be like?"

Without looking up I sensed a nodding of heads before they settled in to the task of writing. This apparent agreement that the request was a reasonable one puzzled me, but then graduate students are a docile lot. They scribbled away for five or six minutes until I stopped them and asked them to pass the papers up to the desk.

I read the sheaf of papers slowly while (I presume) the authors of them watched me closely. Now for the first time I looked up at them. They were really a rather pleasant bunch. I stood up and moved around to the front of the desk, leaned back, sat on the edge, crossed my legs, and smiled pleasantly at them. This last action scared the wits out of them. They had grown so used to the grim, unsmiling, monotonic pedant that they were deeply disturbed by a smile. I think they suspected a malevolent twist in the proceedings.

"This course," I announced in my friendliest manner, "is the book you have begun to 'read,' and I am the narrator." I was animated, outgoing, careful to emphasize important words like "book" and "read." They eyed me warily between scratches at their notebooks. They seemed less comfortable with this turn of events than they had been with the monomaniacal professor who had now evidently gone off somewhere.

"You have been responding to me according to the persona— the narrator—I have been presenting. Let me read to you what you have written." As I had seen right away, those notes about their expectations were revealing and—more interesting—uniformly respectful of the Teutonic Herr Doktor Professor who had been haranguing them for twenty minutes:

"This class will be clearly structured and informative, the instructor probably demanding but interesting."

"The instructor is very professional. He has high standards."

"I am going to have to work very hard in this course, but it will be worth it."

That they might not wish to submit themselves for a semester to the dull martinet who had been reading off book publishers, publication dates, and international book numbers did not seem to occur to them.

I went on reading:

"The instructor does not make much eye contact." (Now there's a nervy graduate student. Still, it was a hedged bet: I hadn't made *any* eye contact.)

The entire batch of ten responses was along these lines. What I found hard to believe was that my research assistant's paper was indistinguishable from the rest. Afterwards, I asked her if she had not wondered at this Mr. Hyde emerging when she had grown accustomed to kindly old Dr. Jekyll. "Yes," she said, "but you scared me."

To be honest, I had scared them all. It took me almost a month before they would accept the possibility that the new narrator—this friendly, cheerful avuncular professor—was the real me. A few of them never did relax—whenever I smiled, they cringed—and waited nervously for the return of Mr. Hyde.

In the semesters that followed I got a lot of mileage out of this experiment by describing it to other classes in the novel when I wanted to make the point about readers and narrators. But you know how it is—I could not resist returning to the scene of the crime.

A few years later I was scheduled to teach the same course, this time at the university's extension center in Kansas City. Why not? I thought. It has been a long time since Mr. Hyde showed his fangs. Older students taking night classes will not have heard of what happened on the Lawrence campus in the distant past.

On the first night I walked into that Kansas City classroom where twenty-five mature men and women awaited the opening session of The English Novel: Readers and Narrators. I sat at the desk, I announced the course, I read out the book list and the reserve list, all in a studied monotone. In short, I repeated the boring performance of five years before, complete with the staccato rendition of passages from the still grim German translation. It took longer to read off twenty-five names than to read off ten, but I was just as dull as I had ever been—maybe duller. An occasional surreptitious glance at the class revealed that they too were writing everything down, although I thought I spied a doubtful look or two cast at me.

When I asked them to take out a sheet of paper, there was the same familiar collective shudder. I told them what I wanted, and they set about writing down their expectations.

About three minutes into this exercise I became aware of some movement toward the back of the room. I peeked. A stout, middle-aged woman had stopped writing and was looking around speculatively. Suddenly, she reached a decision. She closed her notebook, capped her pen, gathered her books, stood up, and walked out.

I was horrified.

Later, I read back their papers to them, but it was clear that this was nowhere near as docile a group as the earlier one. They were not all that sure that this *was* going to be a satisfactory course. A few even had a suspicion that there might be something odd going on. "Is this comment sheet," one of them had written, "a test of our differing reactions to the same phenomenon?"

I had now reached the point where I was sitting on the desk and smiling at them. They accepted this personality change much more easily than the group five years before.

"What made you think," I asked them, "that it might be a trick?"

One of the bolder students responded that, as a teacher herself (and many of them nodded with her), she could not believe that anyone teaching at the university could be *that* bad. I was going to pass this compliment on to my dean until I recalled the one departed student who had evidently decided that she *could* tell a book by its cover. I mentioned her exit, but no one in the now-jolly class had observed it.

We watched together the following week to see if she would return. She never did.

And it was I who waited in fear and trembling week after week to see if my dean would ever discover how, in a time of decreasing enrollments and frenetic efforts to attract nontraditional students, one of his dotty professors had scared a live body, a warm "full-time equivalent," right out of the classroom on opening night.

I swore off all innovation forever and managed to locate my yellowed notes in an old carton where, save for a few easily interpreted mouse tracks, they were none the worse for wear.

SATIRE À LA SARTRE

Even after twenty years of teaching I cannot explain why some classes are special. The right combination of students and teacher, a spark to ignite—whoosh! and off we go. Every professor, I suppose, has, tucked away in a corner of his mind, an image of himself as Mark Hopkins on one end of the log with a receptive student on the other. It never works out like that.

Take my Honors Proseminar in Satire, for example. I don't mean the group which toured the art museum while their wounded professor smiled bravely from his stretcher. No, this group assembled a few years later. There were English majors and computer buffs, a couple of art history students, a journalist, a poet, and a few walk-ons: eleven individuals who wanted to read Swift, Voltaire, Orwell, and the rest.

Or so I thought. Some teachers undoubtedly attract students by reputation or force of personality; evidently, I acquire them by accident. About a month into the semester I was discussing with one of my Satire students the embarrassing number of simple spelling errors in his first paper.

"I know," he answered penitently. "I'm dyslexic."

Naturally, I was sympathetic and assured him that we could work out something. He was pleased and added that actually dyslexia was not always a bad thing. Puzzled, I asked him to explain.

"Well," he said, "when I read the Timetable of Courses, I thought you were teaching an Honors Proseminar in Sartre. It sounded pretty interesting."

"But didn't you wonder at the first few periods on *Mac Flecknoe* and *Gulliver's Travels?*"

"Yes," he admitted. "I could see it would be a long time before you got to Sartre, but I really liked Dryden and Swift."

I took it as a compliment. What else could I do? I think Sartre would have understood.

What might have stumped him, however, were the homemade cookies in the brown paper sack. They appeared on my desk one afternoon when I stepped out for a few minutes during a long session of grading. On the outside of an ordinary small sandwich bag someone had written in fat blue lines with a Magic Marker: "Dr. Gold—happy paper grading." Inside were four round chocolate cookies, each about the size of a golf ball. They were sprinkled with what looked like powdered sugar. I examined the sack again, but except for those few words, there was no other writing. The Satire class was the only one for which I was currently grading anything so it was likely the gift came from one of them. But which one?

I picked out a fat cookie and considered popping it in my mouth. Then I sniffed it. I touched the powdered sugar but refrained from licking it. What, I thought, if there is an A student who is getting a C? How do I know what they are really thinking? Would I know confectioner's sugar from cyanide? Soon enough? You get the idea.

I decided to wait until I could ask my honors students about the anonymous donor. When they heard the question, they all smiled benevolently at me, but nobody confessed to being the bashful baker.

Fortunately, I realized that cookies were prohibited on the new diet I had been considering. The brown sack sat untouched on my desk. I finished my grading, reached the end of the semester, and still had not tasted a crumb.

Toward the end of the term my students filled out a teaching evaluation form—better known as "The Student's Revenge." The idea is that the instructor will not see these responses until after grades are in. When that moment finally came, I sat in my office, feet up, the brown sack still amid the debris on my desk. I opened the first of the evaluations. There, buried in the middle of the sheet, was what I had been waiting for. "I baked the cookies," it read, and the student had signed her name. I felt tremendously relieved: I had recorded an A for her. I reached for a stale cookie while I opened the second evaluation.

I had the cookie nearly to my mouth when I read the paralyzing sentence in the second paper: "I sent you the cookies." This was impossible. I grabbed the sheaf of evaluations and raced through them. All but one or two assured me: "I gave you the cookies."

I sighed and emptied the sack into my wastebasket. I know when I've been had.

Of course, I had suspected their special talents earlier in the term. I had recounted the story of the Paper Shredder—the sign at the bottom of my door, the Chomp! Chomp! CHOMP! to accompany the tearing of scrap paper, and even the confetti I emptied in my classroom. They chortled at all the right places, and we went on to more scholarly matters.

The day I realized just how closely they had been attending was the day their papers were due. I stayed away from my office until nearly 5:30. As I unlocked my door, I saw on the floor a few hundred strips of shredded paper. I have to admit my initial confusion: without quite understanding what had happened, I gathered up the scraps of paper and carried them to my desk. There, I found that segments could be fitted together and deciphered. I appeared to be in possession of ten or eleven (it was a little hard to tell) critical essays on ". . . *andide* and *Saint Joan*," "The Innocents in *Volpone* and *Can* . . ." and "Satiri . . . *Travels*." Page numbers helped me piece parts of essays together. Then, fortunately, I realized that all these scraps seemed to be on copier paper: they were not originals. On a hunch, I went to see the departmental secretaries. Grinning widely, they handed me a large envelope filled with the original essays.

Those wags in the proseminar had Xeroxed their essays, shredded the copies, slid them under my door, and given the originals to the secretaries to whom, obviously, they had explained the whole scam. They were learning the lessons of satire exceedingly well.

If the Cookie Caper and the Paper Shredder Reprise showed what they could do when they put their minds to it, the *Catch–22* Uproar revealed them at their spontaneous best. We had finished *Animal Farm* and were in the second period on *Catch–22*, a book they had loved. There came a moment when I slowed in my remarks about satire, corruption, Milo Minderbinder, and the missing morphine packets.

Three students were having a vigorous discussion. Right there in class. In the middle of my lecture! From what I could gather they *were* talking about *Catch–22*, but *still*. I paused and gave them my penetrating stare. The pause was fatal: four students on the other side of the room began to argue among themselves whether Heller was attacking the army or *all* organizations. I looked pointedly from one group of talkers to the other. They ignored me. Someone in the heretofore silent middle offered an opinion to the person next to him. Two students in the front row turned around and disagreed.

The class was now joyously out of control. Around the room three separate but heated arguments were in progress. I heard my Sartre student manage at last to bring Existentialism into it.

After a few minutes the din grew less fearsome, and there were occasional patches of relative calm. I began to wave my arms about. "Hey," I shouted, sounding like a frenetic John Madden in one of those Miller Lite Beer commercials, "hey, I'm the teacher. When do *I* get to talk?"

A few of them glanced up, perplexed. I think they were trying to recall who I was. Gradually, the buzz died down, the varying viewpoints had been aired, and they were now ready to see what I might like to contribute about *Catch–22*. Well, I did put in a few words (it's in my contract), and they listened politely and even took a couple of notes to encourage me.

Later, back in my office, I reflected on those three or four minutes of uncontrolled fragmented arguments, eleven juniors and seniors so exercised about a book that they didn't have time to wait for the professor. It certainly wasn't Mark Hopkins on one end of the log and a student on the other. They had all climbed up on that log, set it spinning wildly until I splashed into the water, and then they had a high old time.

It was the best class I never taught.

THE HAZARDS OF HUMOR

I cannot claim that I had not been warned. Before I returned to graduate school I spent a grim year selling pharmaceuticals—a detail man calling on physicians. Early in our first year the company brought its apprentice salespeople home to Pearl River, New York, for a three-week training program. With the irreverence of youth I had been cutting up in the classroom—a wry comment here, a bit of mugging there—and was suddenly called to task by the no-nonsense training supervisor.

"Do you think that's funny?" he asked. Actually, I did, but, like Dickens' schoolchildren responding to the visiting gentleman, I was pretty sure that "yes" was not the right answer.

"Well," I temporized.

"Do you?" he insisted, fixing me with a steely glare.

My fellow trainees, who had been laughing at my antics, studied their notes and left me twisting slowly in the wind. It was an early lesson in the loneliness of the comic's life as well as in the dangers of not being serious.

Then there were a few sticky moments in graduate school. I never could take Wordsworth seriously, and I had my problems with the prophetic poems of William Blake. I wrote a seminar paper on the dullness of two eighteenth-century plays, one by Joseph Addison, the other by Samuel Johnson, and cavorted around quite a lot at their expense. My professors chided me gently about these "attempts at humor" but otherwise passed me through. "Some day," my mentor said, "some day you are going to get into trouble."

A good many of the tales in this book, of course, reflect the accuracy of his judgment, but the most worrisome example of high-risk humor was a light-hearted piece I wrote for the *Chronicle of Higher Education*. For once succumbing entirely to the dark angel of fiction, I called it "Destabilizing the Classics." My editor altered the title to "Covert Operations in the Literary Classics," a change which might have made a difference.

It went like this:

It was only after I had read my fourth newspaper account of how college students across the country were warmly welcoming recruiters from the Central Intelligence Agency to their campuses that I began to piece things together. Of course! That explained my newest teaching difficulties.

Take my literature classes. The budding Company men and women have some fascinating interpretations.

"Sir," they ask respectfully, "why didn't Hamlet have the ghost checked out?"

They treat my uncomprehending blink with tolerance. "You know, run a background check on him—business acquaintances, past associations, landlords in Elsinore, the whole bit."

Before I have quite digested this, they are further down the trail. "After all," they go on, "we know Hamlet *thinks* the ghost is *his* agent, but . . ."

I cannot let this misreading of the play continue. "Wait! What do you mean the ghost is Hamlet's agent?"

They are puzzled by my slow mental processes. "He tells us, sir. You're always telling us to read the *text*."

"But . . ."

"It's right there in the first act when the ghost is trying to get him to swear, and Hamlet answers, 'Well said, old mole.'"

Stunned somewhat by their close reading, I try to focus the discussion on Hamlet's moral dilemma—does the ghost come from Hell or is it really the spirit of his dead father? They want to talk about the details of the debriefing operation. I manage to shift their interest to the ending: "Does Hamlet delay too long before he kills the king?"

They are now arguing amongst themselves about what *kind* of poison was on the tip of the sword. Apparently, you can pick up some really good buys down the road in Copenhagen. Just when

I think I have appealed to their aesthetic sensibilities with Horatio's "Good night, sweet prince," I discover that they are much more exercised over Fortinbras marching in with his troops.

"Pretty cool move," they remark admiringly.

"Right. Fix it so that everything's rotten in Denmark and then, whap, a coup. That Fortinbras is one smart operator."

What they don't understand, it turns out, is why the play is called *Hamlet*. *Fortinbras* sounds like a more logical title.

All the classics are grist for the new pragmatism.

For instance, after reading *Oedipus Rex*, they assure me that it would have been an easy assignment to set up old King Laius at the crossroads, a simple covert operation, and that's it. They are especially impressed, they tell me, with the undercover agent. My bewilderment is obvious, and they pity me.

"The agent, sir. To get Oedipus into the palace, actually to make him king. Tremendous field work!"

"But the ending," I splutter. "Oedipus reveals himself as the murderer. How do you explain that?"

They are not fazed. "Well, you see, sir, if his cover has been blown, he might as well make a big deal of it. Then the other agent can stay in place."

"The other agent?"

"The old blind guy. What's his name."

"Teiresias?"

"Yes, that's the one. Nobody is going to suspect him after Oedipus has his big scene."

But it isn't only the serious works which reveal the new mood on campus. Even *Alice in Wonderland* comes in for close scrutiny. If I had been more alert I might have predicted the flap over the Red Queen. But I don't see how I could have guessed their suspicions about the Cheshire Cat.

"He knows more than he's letting on," they insist.

"That smile is a dead giveaway."

"Yeah, and what about the unexplained disappearances? Where

does he go, and who does he see? There's something fishy about that cat."

I thought I had lured them back to theme and character when I got them halfway through *Jane Eyre*. Oh, sure, they had their suspicions of Rochester, but then, who doesn't? However, when they discovered what Grace Poole was hiding up in the attic, the next thing I knew I was being left out of an animated discussion about the merits of Thornfield Hall as a Safe House. Rochester evidently went way up in their estimation for having secreted wife number one in the upper reaches of Thornfield. I had never heard Grace Poole called a Minder before.

When I tried to interest them in "Ozymandias, King of Kings, / Look on my Works, ye Mighty, and despair!" they seemed quite taken with the "two vast and trunkless legs of stone." I was delighted by their interest.

"Who do you think toppled him, sir?"

"Toppled?"

"Yes, you know, destabilized the government. Was it an inside job, do you think?"

I should note that every time I am unable to provide authoritative responses to such questions, I lose a bit of face with my new students. "No," I have to explain, "I do not know how Magwitch laundered the money he sent to Pip." They find this inattention to crucial detail surprising in a university professor. Take Keats' "Ode to a Nightingale," for example. I was frankly startled by their rapt attention to my sonorous reading:

> My heart aches, and a drowsy numbness pains
> My sense, as though of hemlock I had drunk,
> Or emptied some dull opiate to the drains
> One minute past, and Lethe-wards had sunk.

My activist students of the early seventies would have been groaning about the irrelevance of Keats to Real Life. This group was on the edge of their seats. I scored a minor point when I explained that Lethe-wards suggested oblivion, but I squandered it all when they wanted to know just what the drug was. "Did I think it was sodium pent?"

"Pent?"

"Sodium pentothal, sir. Truth serum."

The spirited discussion found me lagging pitifully far behind. They considered some alternative possibilities, analyzed carefully the effects described in the poem—chest pains, sleepiness, numbness, unconsciousness. I suppose I should have been pleased at their deep involvement with the poem, but I felt a pang of envy at being locked out.

Trying to recoup my losses, I pointed out how "some dull opi- ate" matches the sound to the sense. I have bored generations of students with this old chestnut, but the new crowd was interested. They wanted more. I intoned from memory Tennyson's "moan of doves in immemorial elms / And murmuring of innumerable bees." They leaned forward, straining the buttons holding their collars down.

"Would you repeat that, sir?"

Have I ever refused? They were taking notes. Then they wanted to know if there were studies to show how rapidly a subject could be rendered unconscious by a voice droning poetry. Had I ever timed my students to see how long it was before they nodded off?

Certainly not!

They are so earnest and so genuinely interested in the works that it is silly to be irritated. What is difficult is figuring out what will appeal to them and what will not. I thought they would like Dylan Thomas's "Do not go gentle into that good night"—even Mr. Gordon had seemed to like it—but once I rejected their interpre- tation that the poem was written in code, they began thumbing through the other Thomas poems in the anthology. Suddenly the classroom came alive. They had found one that spoke *to them*. I should have known.

They were shouting the lines to each other across the room:

"The force . . ." cried one side of the room.

". . . that through the green fuse . . ."

They began deconstructing the poem—dismantling is probably the more accurate term—right then and there. ". . . that blasts the roots of trees . . ." I was left to take notes. You would be amazed at how much I learned about plastics, gelignite, sensors, and electrical detonators.

The information, of course, is not much help in my teaching, but it's invaluable when it comes to writing letters of recommendation for my recruited students.

Only the most literal-minded of readers could possibly consider such material anything but invention. What I did not reckon on, however, was the semi-annual index for the *Chronicle of Higher Education*, an attempt to classify articles under all the appropriate topics.

Immodestly, but naturally, I looked myself up in the *Chronicle* index. There I was, listed for the classroom spoof as well as for an earlier narrative about my ingenuous encounters with the IRS. I was a bit flurried to find this latter essay listed again under TAXES (See also FINANCES). It would probably cause no harm, but one does not really wish to call attention to oneself under TAXES.

Wondering where else I might find "Covert Operations in the Literary Classics," I riffled aimlessly through the index. LITERA-TURE—good, very good. What scholar would not wish to be indexed under LITERATURE? STUDENTS—logical enough. JOB MARKET, STUDENTS—well, really. But when I considered the entry from the indexer's point of view, I could see the connection, although the humor seemed to have been a distinct casualty. I scanned a few more headings. And then I saw it under the bold, black type: CENTRAL INTELLIGENCE AGENCY. Surely my friends at the *Chronicle* wouldn't do this to me. If I and everyone else turn initially to the index to see if our names appear, what are the chances of the CIA being any different? More likely, they would have eagle-eyed researchers going through systematically, inserting items into their own computers, cross-matching entries, and

turning up all sorts of sinister connections. If I had been mildly unhappy to attract the possible attentions of the IRS, you can imagine how I felt about the prospect of drawing the close scrutiny of the CIA.

The month after the index appeared was a rough one. Any time the university telephone system malfunctioned—with chilling regularity in fact—and my "Hello" was met by a few seconds of silence and then an ominous click, I envisioned banks of tape recorders leaping into action somewhere in northern Virginia. Fearing a honey trap at the Modern Language Association convention, I refused an invitation to coffee from a pleasant Chaucerian I had just met. She backed off nervously when I glanced under the shade of a nearby floorlamp. "Microphones," I said.

After a shaky period my anxieties eased, and I no longer checked to see if my files had been disturbed. (Given the world-class clutter in my office, I was probably safer than most.) But I am positive that in an office deep in the complex at Langley there is a folder with my name on it and my article in it. And probably manning the Internal Surveillance Desk, monitoring the incriminating reports, is my old trainer from the pharmaceutical company.

"No, sir," I mumble penitently. "No, sir, I don't think that's funny at all."

RESEARCH CAPERS

THE TWO CULTURES
AND DR. FRANKLIN'S FLY

About thirty years ago C. P. Snow published a provocative little book decrying the separation of science and the humanities into "The Two Cultures." Committed as I already was to the study of English literature, I lamented the inability of scientists and humanists to discuss ideas together but went on happily burrowing into my own eighteenth-century niche. Little did I realize that a crumbling manuscript letter dated 1796 would lead me into that no-man's land between the two cultures.

Even now, as I sit here in my office, staring at three apparently very dead flies floating—sunk actually—in a stoppered vial of Madeira, I marvel at the innocence with which it all began. I was writing a short article for one of the journals—they usually have "philology" or "philological" in the title—which publish humanists' work. To explain how I found myself between the two cultures, I had better lay out the main points of that essay. (And don't think I mind opening up my arcane researches to more than the half dozen or so scholarly souls who actually read the articles in such journals.)

Near the end of the eighteenth century a man who had been a dinner guest at Benjamin Franklin's French residence related the following anecdote in a letter:

I remember one Day at Dinner, with Doctor Franklin at Passy, in the Year 1779, the Doctor produced a Fly, which had come out of a But of Madeira that Morning, and which by laying in the Sun was restored to Life.—The Doctor wish'd, that he cou'd, in like Manner, be bung'd up for fifty Years, and then restored to Life, to behold the flourishing State, in which America wou'd then be.

Naturally I wondered if others knew of this fey after-dinner story, and I began to poke around in a few books on Franklin. Without really expecting to find anything helpful, I glanced at the index to Carl Van Doren's massive biography and was startled by the entry "Flies drowned in wine, BF on, 431." Back in 1773, some six years before the Passy dinner party, Franklin was writing from London about experiments designed to recall the dead to life. What was most intriguing, however, was a carefully detailed description of drowned flies. Three of them had fallen out of a Virginia-bottled Madeira into a glass. Ever the scientific inquirer, Franklin proposed an experiment to test whether or not the sun could indeed revive drowned flies. Within a few hours two of the three began to stir. Franklin's phrasing is rather stirring itself:

> They commenced by some convulsive motions of the thighs, and at length they raised themselves upon their legs, wiped their eyes with their fore feet, beat and brushed their wings with their hind feet, and soon after began to fly, finding them- selves in Old England, without knowing how they came thither. The third continued lifeless till sunset, when, losing all hopes of him, he was thrown away.

Franklin went on to wish such preservation were possible for hu- mans, "for having a very ardent desire to see and observe the state of America a hundred years hence, I should prefer to any ordinary death, the being immersed in a cask of Madeira wine, with a few friends, till that time, to be then recalled to life by the solar warmth of my dear country!"

It seemed likely to me that puckish Dr. Franklin had carried out his experiment in London in 1773 and then, for the amusement of his dinner guests at Passy six years later, produced a docile fly whose "revivification" allowed him to offer some "spontaneous" conjectures on coming back to see the flourishing state of Amer- ica in fifty years. And so I wrote it up—a little Franklin anecdote for the delectation of my fellow philologists.

If I had been able to leave it at that, I would never have found myself between the two cultures.

I mentioned the flies-in-Madeira to a fellow humanist at a wine and cheese party. (It might not have been in very good taste, but you *can* see how the topic might come up.) "But is that possible?" he asked.

"Is what possible?"

"Can a fly drowned in wine be revived by drying it in the sun?"

Well, of course, I didn't know. Nor did he. Nor did anyone else at our single-culture cocktail party. My curiosity piqued, I decided to conduct a somewhat more extensive investigation on Monday.

The first phone calls were the worst. "Do you have a fly specialist," I asked the receptionist in the Entomology Department. She thought a moment.

"I don't think so. Not flies precisely. But we do have a bee man and a cockroach man. Do you want either of them?"

I guess it was the unpleasant thought of cockroaches in Madeira that led me to ask for the bee man. She rang his number.

Beginnings have always been difficult for me. "I know you're a specialist in bees," I started, "but do you know anything about flies?"

"Who *is* this anyway?" he growled.

"Gold, English Department."

"Oh," he answered with what I, oversensitized I'm sure, took to be a sneer. "Well, I suppose I know something about flies." (Probably compared to any dithering English professor.)

I didn't help the image at all when I launched into my question about whether or not drowned flies could be recalled to life. He sputtered. "This is a joke, isn't it? Perkins, is that you?"

When I finally got the whole Benjamin Franklin—Madeira—America story laid out, he said, "That Franklin always was a wag, wasn't he?" thus indicating that he was a whole lot closer to bridging the gap between the two cultures than I was ever likely to be. "Look," he said, "I don't think it can be done, but why don't you call my friend Baxter, who specializes in drosophilae." By this time

I think he had accurately gauged the quality of his inquirer, and he added quickly—before the pause grew even the slightest bit awkward—"fruit flies." I appreciated the help. "They may," he concluded, "be closer than bees."

I thanked him, reflecting that if fruit flies weren't closer than bees, they were a darn sight nearer than cockroaches. I called the fruit-fly man. "Not fruit flies," he said witheringly. "Drosophilae."

"I beg your pardon."

"Drosophilae! D-r-o- "

I explained that I was in the English Department and spelling was not my problem. (You can see that my morning had made me a mite testy.) I explained the purpose of my phone call. He whooped. There is simply no other term for what he did into that telephone. He whooped.

Then, maybe because he had read C. P. Snow years ago and because he wanted to reach out to his less fortunate brethren in the humanities, he offered what he assumed was a helping hand. "If they were larvae, they could have grown anaerobically."

It was my turn for the pregnant pause. "Right," I said slowly, "just what do *you* mean when you use the word 'anaerobically'?" (a master stroke, implying, of course, that I was quite familiar with the word when used by *my* colleagues—say of Milton's Satan in the burning lake).

His measured response, which I suspected had been heard by generations of freshmen in Biology 101, told me that my master stroke hadn't fooled anyone. "An-ae-robi-cal-ly," he said (coming as close to spelling it as one could come without actually spelling it), "without air." He went on patiently: "If the flies were larvae, they might not have needed oxygen."

I read him the part where Franklin's anthropomorphic (*anaerobic*, indeed!) flies moved their "thighs" convulsively, "wiped their eyes with their fore feet," and so forth. "No," he agreed, "they don't sound like larvae to me. They don't sound like flies either, but I guess you don't care about that."

I cared, but I was damned if I was going to waste any more time with a fruit-fly freak. The cockroach man at least worked with larger creatures. Cockroaches, I thought, probably do have thighs and the rest of the apparatus. It was, however, all I could do to get quit of my now-cavorting scientist. "What are you working on?" he chortled. *"The Lord of the Flies?"* I knew I was driving another spike between the two cultures, but it *was* satisfying to hang up on Baxter the Fruit Fly.

I hesitated only a little before dialing the cockroach man. After all, I thought, the Kafka specialists probably call him all the time. When I got through to his lab, however, I learned that he was in South America and would be gone for a year. If it was urgent, the secretary said (I considered briefly the kind of "urgent" calls a cockroach man would be getting), I might want to talk to his research assistant. The research assistant had a pleasant, sunny voice, and I found it easy to tell her the story of Dr. Franklin and the flies. I found her giggles much more encouraging than the disbelieving snorts of my first two scientists. I told her that I had talked to the bee expert and the drosophilist but that neither had seemed to understand. "No, I suppose not," she answered cryptically. When I asked her what she thought about the possibility that Franklin had actually revived his drowned flies, her response convinced me that I had finally found a kindred spirit: "We *could* try an experiment," she said. How marvelous that "we" sounded to me: I had been out there on the fringe alone for so long. And "experiment" sounded so, well, so scientific. I felt as if I had thrown my first bridge across the culture gap.

"What kind of experiment?"

"Leave it to me," she said.

About a week later I opened my office door and immediately sensed something new in the room, some intruder among the dusty books, unfiled notecards, and ungraded term papers. There was a stoppered vial of amber liquid sitting on my desk. A closer inspection revealed a tag around the sealed bottle top that read: "Contents: 3 adult *M. domestica* in 100 cc Paul Masson Madeira." Inside were three very dead—or very stoned, I amended with a bow to my new-found scientific spirit—flies.

There was an eight-and-a-half-by-eleven piece of paper under

the vial. It was a dittoed experiment sheet with space for details to be entered, and its very format, its specific categories, seemed to lend an aura of legitimacy and significance to my search for Truth:

Experimenter:
Date:
Pheromone Type: [whatever that meant]
Species:
Sample #:
Test: Qual.:
Dilutions:
    $C_0 =$
        Serial:
Test Results:
Sample History:
Comments:

Even as I scanned that impressive form and sloshed the Madeira around a bit (setting up an interesting spiraling motion among the floating *M. domestica*), I could not help thinking how unmethodical we humanists were. There must be a way to study *Hamlet* or *Paradise Lost* or *The Faerie Queene* more systematically.

Then I began to examine the entries made by my research assistant (how easily I appropriated her services; but the cockroach man *was* in South America). The "Sample," I saw, consisted of "3 living adult *M. domestica*" (how she knew they were adult I did not know), which, I learned under "Sample History," had been caught in Room 125 Snow Hall. Apparently janitorial service was no better in Snow Hall than it was in the Humanities Building. Somehow that thought pleased me. The Paul Masson Madeira had been purchased at a local liquor store, I saw, but its Previous History was "Unknown."

If I was beginning to show signs of a new scientific spirit, I suspected that my research assistant was crossing cultural boundaries too. One of her entries went well beyond the requirements of the form. It was exactly the kind of gratuitous tidbit I usually tucked away in footnotes to philological essays. Quoting from the bottle label, she had written, "This wine has a taste as rich as its place in early American history." How Benjamin Franklin would have loved that! Had Paul Masson known Dr. Franklin in France? No, no, there would be time enough for such questions when this experiment was finished.

The Test Results were to be determined by me. And what were we testing? The "possible reviviscence of *M. domestica* bottled in Madeira; said *M. domestica* to be removed from wine two months hence." For the next few weeks I examined the vial daily, observing the total inactivity of the inhabitants and the unpleasant way the glass had of magnifying their size. One of the departmental secretaries spotted the amber vial and came in for a closer look. She went out quickly and has refused to type anything for me since. Another secretary took to visiting my office and announcing for all to hear: "I've come to look at your fly." I seemed to be bridging two cultures, but they weren't science and humanism. I also noticed that I was spending considerably less time advising students. Sitting in the chair opposite me, asking about what course in social science or mathematics they needed, their eyes would be caught by a glint of light on the amber vial. They would look quickly back at me, but from then on it was only a matter of time before they were staring at those dead flies and suddenly remembering a class meeting or a doctor's appointment. I tried to explain the vial to one bright student, but she said it was all right—she understood. She worked summers at the state mental hospital.

As a matter of fact, none of this has turned out as I thought it would. After the article appeared in *Modern Philology*, my own colleagues got a bit sniffy. They muttered about professional standards. Then, when they saw the flies in my office, they muttered about housekeeping standards. Nor could I bring myself to unseal the vial. I watched and I brooded. As fewer and fewer professors of literature would pass the time of day with me, I began phoning Professor Baxter—you remember the fruit-fly freak?—over in entomology. Baxter turned out to be rather a good sort and was quite interested when he heard I actually had an experiment brewing. After a few informative and pleasant phone conversations, we have taken to visiting each other. I go to his lab or he comes over here, and we discuss his flies or mine or Ben Franklin's—over a glass of aged Madeira, naturally.

SEDUCED BY SCHOLARSHIP

I don't know how the "publish-or-perish" myth got started. Supposedly, professors who do not engage in fruitful research will wither on the academic vine. The truth is that poking around, asking questions about literature, historical events, or even drowned flies, is good fun and often irresistible. You can never tell when you will be snared by a mystery, caught up in the long-buried lives of ordinary people, or swept off to some remote and quaint locale on the scholarly trail. I think the process is what keeps scholars *from* perishing. I can imagine few greater pleasures than to catch a glimmer of a puzzle to be solved or history to be unearthed and then to gallop off on a hobbyhorse, hallooing after the little foxes and wild hares which inhabit the underbrush of literature.

Let me offer an example. For an edition of the letters of John Wilkes, a prominent (perhaps "notorious" is a better word) eighteenth-century British politician, I had been sifting through crumbling materials in the Public Record Office in Chancery Lane, London, systematically unwrapping scores of dusty affidavits from the Court of King's Bench for the year 1763. Almost.before I knew it, I found myself caught in the web once more.

It seems that Mrs. Layng—Mrs. George Layng of Chamberlain Street in the city of Wells—was "lying in," awaiting the house call of Benjamin Pulsford, surgeon and midwife. A nurse attending Mrs. Layng testified that on the ninth of December Benjamin Pulsford knocked on the kitchen window and asked her to bring a chair outside because he could not stand. He was "greatly afflicted and much crippled with the gout." When the nurse came outside with the chair, she discovered the immediate cause of Pulsford's difficulties. There, she attested, was Barclay Cope, Gentleman (but apparently not much of one), "standing against the wall of the said house between the door thereof and the said kitchen window with an intent or purpose . . . to prevent the said Benjamin Pulsford from leaning or supporting himself against the said wall."

I shuffled through the pile of affidavits until I found Pulsford's deposition. He claimed that Cope had "abused" him "with the most scurrilous names and language" and had attempted shoving him "into the cartway and throwing him down."

But why? Why would anyone treat poor Mr. Pulsford in such a mean-spirited way? What had led these two men to the showdown on Chamberlain Street? Was the answer among the few remaining unwrapped affidavits? It was.

A year and a half earlier—fittingly enough on the first of April— Pulsford, Cope, and several other persons were "engaged at cards, at a game called whist." Like a character in an eighteenth-century comedy, Barclay Cope turned out to be "a native of the kingdom of Ireland and officer in the army," who had lived in Wells for a number of years.

In the course of this friendly game, Pulsford and his partner perceived that Barclay Cope, one of their opponents, had "renounced or reneged"—failed to follow suit when he was able— and Pulsford "insisted on his forfeiting three tricks or lifts as is usual in that game." Not content with his three-trick penalty, Benjamin Pulsford could not resist a bit of raillery. According to Pulsford himself, he said "in a jocular and amiable manner, without any the least intention or apprehension of affronting or displeasing the said Barclay Cope, that no good did come of cheating or that cheating did not prosper, or to that purpose or effect."

Apparently, those were fighting words in eighteenth-century Wells, just as they would have been in nineteenth-century Dodge. Barclay Cope responded "instantly" and told Pulsford that he "lied." Then Cope "rose from his seat and advanced" on Pulsford "in great choler and anger and further told him that he . . . would have satisfaction." From these "words or expressions," Pulsford concluded that Cope "meant to fight with him . . . either with swords or pistols."

Well! That would certainly dampen one's interest in continuing the whist game or in making *any* kind of remark "in a free and jocular manner" to a native of Ireland, an officer and a gentleman. But now the motive was clear: Barclay Cope's behavior on Chamberlain Street a year and a half later was probably connected to the earlier altercation.

By this time the scholarly seduction had evolved into a full-blown affair. The Public Record Office could not make photocopies of the fragile documents, but I was allowed to sit in an isolated office and read into a tape recorder all the events and characterizations set forth on those two-hundred-year-old affidavits. What all this had to do with John Wilkes, the ostensible subject of my research, I had no idea. I filled a couple of tapes, retied all the bundles, and carried my recorded treasure across the Atlantic.

Unfortunately, as often happens to researchers, I could find no satisfying final judgment. I guess I was looking for one of those "Crime-Does-Not-Pay" postscripts which used to conclude the old "Gangbusters" or "Dragnet" radio series: "On 21 December in the fourth year of the reign of King George III, Barclay Cope, Gentleman, was sentenced to three months in Bridewell Prison." But there was nothing. Even the archivists at the P.R.O. drew a blank when I wrote and asked for more information. I felt as if I had missed the last few minutes of *Witness for the Prosecution*.

John Wilkes, who lured me into all those affidavits and tangled lives, has led me down other slippery paths. A radical Member of Parliament for Aylesbury, he had attacked George III in a number of pamphlets, had printed an abbreviated, pornographic version of Alexander Pope's *Essay on Man* (the *Essay on Woman*, of course), and had been convicted of sedition and obscenity.

Such a character can bring a scholar into difficulties. One semester when I was a visiting assistant professor at Bowling Green in Ohio, I needed a copy of the *Essay on Woman*, but there was none at the university library. No problem, I thought: I shall simply write to Special Collections at Kansas and ask for a photocopy of theirs. Three weeks passed. How long can it take to copy a 94-line obscene poem? About a week later, the copy finally arrived with an apology for the delay. One look at the steamy material she was being asked to duplicate had been enough for the regular operator of the copying machine. She refused. So late at night, after everyone else had left the library, the Head of Special Collections had been quietly photocopying the *Essay on Woman* for me. For a paper I was to read at a scholarly conference in Chicago, I analyzed the poem and sprinkled my text with a few lubricious quotations. I was prepared to deliver it with panache. Looking up as I read my first suggestive sentence to the audience, I was startled to see, among my cynical and jaded colleagues, two smiling and attentive nuns dressed in the old-style black. Badly shaken by my awareness of what was to follow in my *explication de texte*, I stumbled back into my opening paragraph. They listened quietly throughout the paper, murmuring occasionally to each other, and taking a distressing number of notes. At the conclusion both of them came up to tell me how much they had learned from my talk. I hardly knew how to respond. They blessed me before moving off to the next session.

After that experience I kept my Wilkes researches pretty much under cover. A few years later, however, at a meeting of the Johnson Society of London, I thought I had found some kindred spirits. Two dozen clubbable Johnsonians had assembled at a small hotel on Bloomsbury Square to hear a talk on John Wilkes, the very man whose letters I was reading day in and day out in the Manuscript Reading Room of the British Library. Even better, the speaker was a knowledgeable librarian with impeccable scholarly credentials. Wilkes and I were about to emerge from the closet. I began to formulate a few spontaneous comments for the question period to follow. I thought I would sit back, let someone else open the discussion, and then offer my cogent impromptu remarks.

A distinguished-looking gentleman with long white hair and a florid face raised his hand. From the moment he began to talk to the moment he ceased, he had not a single good word for Wilkes or the now-cringing speaker. First, the sharp-tongued gentleman expounded on Wilkes' immorality and political opportunism; then he went on to lament the sheer waste of time and intellectual

energy spent in studying such an arrant rascal. When this ten-minute diatribe subsided, nobody else seemed much inclined to add anything. Indeed, we were all quietly studying our programs or the backs of our hands. I thought I would save my remarks for another occasion.

It was years before that moment came, but when it did, the call was crystal clear. For a session at the Modern Language Association meetings in Los Angeles in 1982, the announced topic was "Rakes, Rogues, Reprobates, and Renegades in the Enlightened Age." Here I was with *the* rake, rogue, reprobate, and renegade of the century! What a tremendous sense of relief I felt to let out all those spontaneous remarks I had been storing since that afternoon on Bloomsbury Square. I really made the case for John Wilkes as a four-letter man—four R man actually—and I ignored, without compunction, in the question period which followed, the raised hands of the two nuns in the front row. Why push my luck?

To acquire the evidence for that MLA paper I had followed the siren song of scholarship to a few eighteenth-century dens of iniquity. As the choleric critic at the Johnson Society had observed, Wilkes had been notorious, at least early in his career, for immorality. The young Wilkes had been an active member of a Hellfire Club, a loose organization—I kid you not—of young bucks who met to celebrate carnal delights and black masses—in whichever order the spirits moved them.

Most of their orgies occurred on the site of old ruined Medmenham Abbey, but a few supposedly took place in some salt and limestone caves at West Wycombe in Buckinghamshire. Tourist-minded restorers have furnished rooms in the caves with wax models of the original players celebrating their favorite pastimes—a risqué underground Madame Tussaud's. My research has taken me to some strange places, but none stranger than the caves of West Wycombe. As my wife and I edged slowly along a pathway which grew more narrow and more slippery the deeper we went, I could not help wondering if my sedate colleagues who specialize in Shakespeare and Milton would be descending to such levels. (An unworthy pun, I know, but my brain was growing chilled.) Every twenty steps seemed to drop the temperature another ten degrees. Finally, we reached the alleged scene of the alleged carryings-on of two centuries ago. Shivering, we peered at the wax figures frozen in their frolics. My wife, who was now wearing my sports jacket and my raincoat, offered the definitive judgment:

"I d-d-d-don't b-b-believe it w-w-w-would be p-p-p-possible to have an or-g-g-gy d-d-down here."

When we surfaced again, and I had reacquired my warm clothing, I vowed to confine my researches to libraries and archives. Caves were definitely off limits.

Led on by my need to locate all the Wilkes letters still in existence, I scrutinized whatever library and archive catalogues I could find. A computer printout of all the historical manuscript letters in Great Britain turned up a listing for seventy-five Wilkes letters in the Buckinghamshire Archaeological Society at Aylesbury. I was surprised at this entry because I thought I had, by this time, found the important holdings of manuscript letters. I wrote a brief note to the Archaeological Society, explaining that I would be in Aylesbury a week from the current date and "would like to examine your Wilkes material." The following Tuesday, after a pleasant hour's drive up from London, I arrived at the door of the Archaeological Society's rambling seventeenth-century house.

A cheerful, middle-aged lady sitting just inside the front door was delighted to see me.

"You must be Professor Gold," she said. "We received your letter last week, and, if you will follow me, I'll take you to the Wilkes material."

Impressed by the crisp efficiency with which my request had been handled, I followed dutifully through a series of rooms, up a rickety staircase, and into a chamber which looked like a repository for lost umbrellas, scarred end tables, and other unwanted bric-a-brac. She brought me to a desk and asked me to wait.

"I'll only be a moment," she said.

One of the symptoms of those who quest for the scholarly grail is a rising sense of anticipation, an elevation of the pulse, at the imminent appearance of old manuscripts or rare books. I tried to control my excitement as I heard her footsteps returning. The cheerful lady was carrying a large round object which she proudly placed on the desk in front of me. I stared at it without comprehension.

"It's rather attractive, don't you think?"

I murmured some words of assent and picked up what appeared to be a large china bowl with blue figures and the legend "Wilkes and Liberty!" inscribed around the circumference. I turned the bowl. On the other side were the numbers "1763," the date of Wilkes' attack on George III and the government in his pamphlet, *The North Briton*. I understood. What I was holding was one of the thousands of souvenirs produced by the enterprising to celebrate Wilkes' notoriety. The lady from the Archaeological Society was beaming as she handed me a ceramic mug bearing the same inscription.

"This is one of our treasures," she said.

I admired it as it deserved. There were a few more bowls, mugs, and silver tankards, all of which I admired to her satisfaction. Finally, I had to ask.

"But where are the letters by Wilkes?"

"The letters?"

I explained about the printout and the seventy-five manuscript letters which were supposed to be here.

"Oh," she said, "when you wrote about wanting to see the

Wilkes materials, I thought. . . ." But she recovered quickly. "If you can return this afternoon I'll have them ready for you."

For the next two hours I sampled the Ploughman's Lunch and the Charrington on tap at the Admiral Byng down the road. Shortly before three I presented myself once more at the Buckinghamshire Archaeological Society. The mishaps of the morning had not diminished my excitement. The ripple of anticipation and the faster pulse came right on schedule. And so, a few minutes later, did the keeper of the treasures, bearing a large carton which contained, she said, "the Wilkes letters you wished to see."

Immediately I dipped into the prize. The first letter was a photocopy, not an original. So was the next and the next. I pulled out the entire stack. They were all copies! I examined a few of them more closely and realized that I had seen these letters somewhere in my travels. The Archaeological Society lady was hovering about, wanting to be sure that I was suitably pleased with the contents.

"They're all photocopies."

"Yes, of course," she said.

It turned out she had no idea where the originals were or why the Historical Manuscripts Commission should have misled me into thinking that the letters at Aylesbury were originals. She was not really surprised when I informed her that the letters were in America, in Ann Arbor, Michigan.

"Hmmm," she sniffed. "I might have known."

Ignoring this hint of chauvinism, I asked if I might skim through the copies to be sure I had recorded them all in my master list of Wilkes letters. So I spent the remaining hours of daylight sorting through the stack of letters. Nearing the bottom, I felt a very different kind of paper. I was amazed to discover that I was holding an original John Wilkes letter dated 1760. There was another one right under it from 1761. I quickly leafed through to the bottom of the carton and then went back over the copies I had already sorted. There were no other originals. I looked carefully at my master list and realized that the two manuscript letters I was holding were not recorded anywhere. Even the Archaeological Society didn't know these two were in the carton. Evidently, when copies were made before sending the originals to the Clements Library in Ann Arbor, these two had slipped back into the box of copies. The Clements was two short, Aylesbury was two long, and I was the only one who knew.

Did I consider slipping those valuable manuscripts into my pocket and walking off into a new life in which I would no longer have to order the Ploughman's Lunch? Did I think about flying the Concorde home to the U.S.A. instead of squeezing aboard a People's Express?

Ah. Well.

In the end I resisted the seductive visions and did not swerve from the scholarly path. As the last rays of sunlight fell across my temporary desk at the Buckinghamshire Archaeological Society, I inscribed in my notebook all the details about the two letters— the dates, the recipients, the place from which they were written— thus assuring future researchers a full record of John Wilkes' correspondence. I would later get my own photocopies of them. I carried the carton back to the desk.

I set it down and solemnly handed the keeper the two manuscript letters. "Oh, dear," she said, "now where did *they* come from." I flashed her a rueful smile, tightened the belt of my trench coat and left her there puzzling over how she was going to explain the sudden appearance of letters long presumed sold.

My virtue intact, I walked out into the Aylesbury dusk.

"Louie," I said to no one in particular, "this could be the start of a beautiful friendship."

THE SHORTHAND MAN

Even when I force myself to resist the lure of dusty affidavits at the Public Record Office, I never seem to come up with a truly Significant Research Topic like Shakespeare's Kings or Sin in *Paradise Lost*. Take my latest project. The fellow across the hall was impressed when he learned I was spanning a hundred and sixty-five years of history.

"That's a major undertaking," he said.

I nodded modestly.

"What are you doing? The development of the novel from *Tom Jones* to *The Mayor of Casterbridge*?" I shook my head.

"Lyric poetry from Blake to Yeats?" No. "The Fallen Woman from Clarissa to Tess of the d'Urbervilles?"

Well, of course, he had to give up. "*What* then?"

"Shorthand books," I announced primly. "Shorthand books from 1635 to 1800." I began to explain why I had chosen these particular years, but he suddenly recalled a student who "was coming by in a few minutes," and he drifted back into his office.

I thought how unfair it all was. I *would* have chosen Donne's sonnets or Shaw's irony if it had been up to me, but sometimes fate or serendipity takes a hand.

I had been spending the summer in Chicago at the Newberry Library, where I was studying Samuel Johnson's English translation of a French version of a Portuguese manuscript of the travels of a seventeenth-century Jesuit into the wilds of Ethiopia. (That's what I mean, about the byways, footpaths, and underbrush of literature.) Anyway, for a project on how speeches were reported my wife had asked me if the Newberry had any books on shorthand.

On a slow afternoon I located the appropriate catalogue drawer and pulled it out, expecting to find a dozen or so titles. The entire drawer was on Shorthand. I examined the label on the outside of the drawer: Shorthand, A-M. I looked at the drawer directly beneath it: Shorthand, N-Z. I had inadvertently stumbled on the second largest collection of shorthand books in the United States. I was intrigued but not impressed. However, as the summer wore on, and books about Ethiopian liturgies began to pall (this occurred about the second or third day), I ordered up a few of the shorthand books just to see what they looked like.

Well, one book led to another, and by the time autumn had come to the near North Side, I had idly taken fifty pages of notes. To my surprise, I was looking forward to each new claim made by the egocentric inventors of shorthand systems: "If a child of eight be set to learning this sytem for fifteen minutes in the morning and fifteen minutes at night," he will be "perfect in it by the age of ten." (And you, too, can learn to play the organ after twenty-five minutes of practice!) I was fascinated by the occasional venom with which one inventor might attack all who had gone before. And just about everyone was a candidate to learn shorthand— students, ministers, attorneys, clerks, travelers, spies. Spies? (Nobody would be able to decipher their scrawls. Unless, I suppose, the counterspy had learned the same system.) So I realized I was hooked. I like to think that anyone would have been, but after all these years I recognize the fatal weakness in my scholarly constitution.

Over the next few years, every time I visited a research library—the Huntington, the Houghton, the New York Public—I examined their shorthand books. The collection at the New York Public Library is the largest in the United States, but it is housed mostly at the Annex—around Tenth Avenue and 43rd Street. I should have known, of course. If it had been Yeats or Swift, Austen or Thackeray, the books would have been up on posh Fifth Avenue, with the long, impressive stairway, the guardian lions, the marble floors. But, "Shorthand books, sir? Try the Annex over by the docks."

Still, I continued to absorb countless interesting facts which nobody else knew. For example, many of the inventors were writing masters who taught shorthand on the side. Some resisted publishing shorthand books because they feared losing pupils if they gave their secrets away in a book. Many of them offered to answer "any reasonable question" for a reader who would write to the author "post paid." Or, they would make house calls to teach "gentlemen or ladies." Carried away at last by all this fascinating material, I volunteered to discuss it at a meeting in Brussels. My university, which pays air fare for its wandering professors to speak at international meetings and spread its fame, saw the title of my proposed paper and offered me two-thirds of the air fare. I took the money.

As soon as my name and subject appeared in the program for the meetings, I began receiving letters from correspondents who had cryptic, possibly coded, sheafs of paper littering their attics. They saw me as a specialist who might possibly unravel old family problems. One English correspondent was on the verge of mailing me a shorthand ledger book which had been lying about his firm's premises for a hundred years. I had to decline for fear of losing my amateur status.

By this time, however, I had grown bold enough to come out of the closet. I shall apply, I thought, for a sabbatical to go to England, where I shall huddle happily over the shorthand books in the British Museum and the University of London library.

When I reached London for a year on half pay, I decided to

increase my expertise by learning to write shorthand. I began thumbing through the London Yellow Pages looking for secretarial colleges or courses. My misgivings multiplied after the first few phone calls. Was the young lady a graduate? Had my daughter taken typing courses? When I explained that *I* was the one who wanted to be taught shorthand, there was a giggle, and then a few words filtered through a hand over the mouthpiece—"Cor! 'ere's a bloke wants to learn shorthand."

There had to be another way. Skimming idly through my local weekly newspaper, I wandered past the classified advertisements for used furniture, massage, electrolysis, and flat-sharing. Under "Instructional Services" just before "Spanish Flamenco" I found it: "Shorthand Lessons—private tutoring." I dialed the telephone number in the ad, and a male cockney accent answered.

Yes, he could teach me shorthand. I explained that I did not have to be proficient in writing quickly: I just wanted to understand it, to read it, and to write a little.

My merely wanting to read and understand shorthand rather than wanting to whiz through dictation produced a long pause. Then he found a way to explain it to himself: "You want to learn the theory, you do." Only he pronounced it "theeee-ry." I agreed, and he told me what supplies to buy: a shorthand notebook, some hard black pencils, and a Pitman *New Era* shorthand book. I hurried over to my local W. H. Smith and received a great deal of assistance from clerks eager to provide my daughter all the right materials for her shorthand course. As long as they were rushing around being helpful, there didn't seem much point in correcting them about the identity of the student.

Back at my flat I sharpened my three new pencils, opened my notebook to the first page, and settled down to Chapter One. Four minutes later I knew this was going to be a breeze. I worked the first exercises in ten minutes, reread the chapter, skimmed Chapter Two, and went to bed secure in my mastery of the rudiments.

At the appointed time the next morning I arrived at my tutor's house. He was a short, round little man, with twinkling eyes and a one-track mind. "You just want to learn the theeee-ry, you do." I heard this twice the first day and at least once in every future interview. I like a man who knows what he's teaching. He showed me how to hold my pencil, praised some of my squiggles and corrected others. He told me he had been a professional short-hand writer for the Ford Motor Company before he retired. Now he took on private pupils, mostly, he said, young girls seeking secretarial jobs. "They need to be fast and accurate, but you," he said happily, "you want to learn the theeee-ry."

Chapter Two and the required writing took a little longer than Chapter One, but I was working well within my intellectual capacities. The next few weeks shook my confidence somewhat. Simple squiggles were giving birth to more complex ones; little dots and circles crept into the lessons, altering sounds and meanings. Where only a fortnight earlier I had been dashing off tough complete sentences like "Abe Page paid the debt" with hardly a thought, I now found that I was not quite making it through the entire assignment before I went to my appointment.

I tried to reason with my teacher. "The chapters," I told him, "are almost twice as long as they were in the beginning. Can't we take two days on one chapter?"

He would not hear of it. The seventeen-year old school leavers were trotted out and praised for their perseverance. I tried to appeal to him as a fellow teacher and urged the educational advantages of slowing down the process. No soap. I pointed out that I was willing to *pay* for two periods of one chapter. No sale. Apparently, one chapter had always equaled one session, and thus it would ever be.

I fell further and further behind. Abe Page's debt had long since been paid. Now it was "The General Iron & Steel Company, 14 Trent Street, Glasgow." And he didn't even say "Glasgow" the way we did in America.

One day while we were struggling with the language barrier—I had been trying to figure out how to write "'eretic" in Pitman's shorthand—he told me he had been to America a few years before. California and Florida, he said. I tried a little joke: "We don't consider California and Florida part of America." He was absolutely stunned.

"But, the travel agent said. . . ."

I decided to soldier on without the jokes. So twice a week I managed one chapter while he was going over two.

To maintain my sense of professionalism I shuffled through cartons and cartons of collected shorthand materials—old books, photographs, certificates of merit, yellowed advertisements—squirreled away for the University of London by a renowned shorthand scholar. Taking copious notes, spending scores of pounds for photocopying, I was able to recover somewhat from feeling myself a lagging schoolboy who had not done his lessons. Here in the Palaeography Room, I thought, here I am clearly a scholar. Unfortunately, a few months into my sojourn in the Palaeography Room I looked up to discover one of the librarians doubtfully shaking her head as she observed me sorting through the dusty relics.

"What is it?" I asked.

"I'm sorry," she said. "But you just don't look like a shorthand man."

I was dead in the water. What does a shorthand man look like? Was I too breezy? Too American?

It was a combination of these and other factors: I should have been much shorter, a bit pudgier, with thicker glasses, and attired in gravy-spattered ascot and waistcoat. I should also, I gathered, have been closer to eighty than forty.

It seemed like a good time to leave London for a while and sample the provinces. So I packed up my hard pencils and my notebooks and took the grand tour to Manchester, Cambridge, Oxford, and Exeter, all repositories of old shorthand books. Then I planned the last scholarly journey of my sabbatical year—an automobile trip to East Germany and storied Dresden, where an almost forgotten collection of early shorthand books was housed.

The drive from London to Dresden by way of Copenhagen, Goslar, and Leipzig and then back by way of Vienna, Salzburg, Heidelberg, and Cologne makes another story, one, I should add, in which the IRS has already expressed great interest. In Dresden, my wife and daughter, a recent high school student of German, dropped me off at the Sächsische Landesbibliothek in the Marien-allee. When I registered at the security post inside the entrance, the guard notified the Stenografische Bibliothek hidden away somewhere in the building, and after a while the librarian to whom I had written came down to collect me. On our journey through the hallways and up the elevator she explained in a com-bination of English and German that the building housed not only the *Bibliothek* but also offices of the Parliament for the state of Saxony.

When we reached the library, she wheeled out a large cart on which, with marvelous efficiency, she had prepared all their short-hand books for the years between 1635 and 1800. With manic in-tensity I scrambled through more than a hundred books in about three hours. After a spirited barrage of "danke schön" and "bitte schön," I was guided back to the security post. Although I was half an hour later than I had expected to be, I knew my family would not panic. They had seen me often enough lost in the stacks of a research library. Occasionally in the heat of a family social gath-ering someone would bring up the hour and a half they had waited in the hot sun outside the Clements Library in Ann Arbor. They would not be fazed by half an hour on a pleasant June day in Dresden.

In the lobby everyone seemed to be staring at me. Not only was the guard inspecting me more carefully than he had done when I entered, but secretaries were coming out of inner offices and peer-ing. "Kurz, kurz," I heard them whisper to each other. I figured it was the special Dresdenian way of saying goodby. I waved at them and called "Auf wiedersehen." They scurried back to their offices.

My family was waiting at the car, more anxious than I would have expected, and when I looked back, there were three or four people standing on the steps of the Sächsische Landesbibliothek waving to us.

As you will have surmised, there was more to the story than

Teutonic friendliness. When I failed to appear at the agreed-upon hour, my daughter, confident in her skills *auf Deutsch*, entered the building to seek out her missing *Vati*. Apparently Kansas German and Dresden German are not quite interchangeable: the guard and all subsequent officials (three, I gathered) denied my ever having been there. She tried to explain to them about the shorthand collection, but she must have been talking to officials of the Parliament.

"Nein, nein," they kept telling her. No such person was in the building. She insisted that I had gone in at ten in the morning, and I had not come out. She did not tell them that I often did not come out of libraries when I was supposed to. Some things do not translate very well.

"Shorthand," she kept repeating.

It was their turn to be worried. They were finally convinced that there was a tall American loose in the Parliament Building, doing *Gott in Himmel* knew what. There must have been some frantic telephone calls and probably a search which was aborted only when I, oblivious, wandered out.

I now realized why they had been whispering when I emerged. "Kurz, kurz," they were saying, and waggling their fingers. And, of course, there on the steps in the Marienallee they were waving goodby to The Man with Short Hands.

It had been a long time coming, but surely there could be no more doubt: I was a Short Hand Man at last.

MEMOIRS OF A LIBRARY COLLECTOR

In my youth I was an avid baseball fan. I collected autographs and scorecards, magazines and bubble-gum cards. It was also my ambition to collect all the major league baseball parks—to see at least one game in every one. Growing up in New York, I had a pretty good head start with Ebbets Field, Yankee Stadium, and the Polo Grounds. On a visit to relatives in Detroit I watched the Tigers play in Briggs Stadium. I traveled to Shibe Park in Philadelphia and up to Fenway in Boston. As an undergraduate in Missouri, I made it to Sportsman's Park to see Stan Musial destroy my New York Giants with five home runs in a doubleheader. As a graduate student I picked up Comiskey Park in Chicago and Crosley Field in Cincinnati, but it was clear that the flame of acquisition was flickering. And besides, it was getting tougher: some of the new ballparks were now out beyond the Rockies.

But old collectors never die, they just shift interests. If graduate school was the last hurrah—a desultory drive to see the Cincinnati Reds—it was the beginning of a new addiction.

It started simply enough. In connection with an eighteenth-century seminar at Indiana I wandered into the Lilly Library; when I went home one spring break I visited the New York Public Library and ignored recently built Shea Stadium; I wrote a letter to the British Museum. By the time I reached Kansas I was hooked. I haunted the Spencer Research Library on campus, went off between semesters to gaze at the dark stones of the Newberry in Chicago, and sat devoutly in the domed reading room of the Library of Congress. I checked in at San Marino and toured the gardens and stacks of the Huntington Library, a civilized place for scholarship if ever there was one. I went east to the Beinecke at Yale, where the reading room looks out at white, rounded sculptures. I returned to New York. The Dodgers and my Giants were

long gone, Ebbetts Field and the Polo Grounds were fading memories, but the magnificent stone lions still stood at Fifth Avenue
and 41st Street, guarding the entrance to the great library. Further
up the steps the derelicts stretched full length, and the young,
finger-snapping music buffs hoisted their hundred-pound blasters
on their shoulders. Inside, you took a ticket, were sent to the North
or South Reading Room, and waited until your number came up
on the electric tote board. It was like Bingo for Books. Weird, un-
bathed characters read or snoozed at adjacent desks. Oh, the
NYPL was—and is—one of the really great ones.

Wherever my eighteenth-century research carried me, I poked
about happily in special collections libraries. I found the Clark in
Los Angeles, the Houghton at Harvard, the Clements in Ann Arbor.
At the Clements, the staff went out for lunch and closed the library
from twelve to one, but they used to lock me in during the lunch
hour—a book and manuscript junkie's dream. Who cared about
Briggs Stadium or Sportsman's Park? Now I had the Clements, the
Boston Public, and rare book libraries at the Universities of Illi-
nois, Minnesota, and Chicago. Plus the New York Public—Main
Branch *and* the Annex! How many scholars had *them*?

Sooner or later, any serious collector of libraries will hear the
siren song from across the Atlantic. And so it was for me. The
professor had never forgotten the thrill the graduate student had
felt on receiving a response from the British Museum. *The* British

Museum in Bloomsbury. How could it ever lose its charm? And there were so many superb research libraries over there—in Great Britain, in France, in Germany. The lure was irresistible.

So I became an international collector, jetting to Paris and the Bibliothèque Nationale, to London and the Guildhall and, of course, the B.M. I wandered to Leiden, journeyed to Cambridge, drove up to Oxford and climbed the stairs to Duke Humfrey at the Bodleian. I scheduled scholarly trips where the libraries were; some tours I planned and then *hoped* there was a research library in the environs. And even as I was accumulating libraries, the Internal Revenue Service was collecting my Employee Business Expenses forms.

"What is Gold doing this time?" they must have wondered. "Grenoble, Besançon, and Avignon. Surely he can provide no valid rationale."

But, of course, each of those stunning cities had a research library or archive, and in those small repositories there was a manuscript letter from or to (why be unduly selective?) John Wilkes. In the mornings I would locate the building, put in my request, wait for the Wilkes letter, and patiently copy out its contents. Then I would blink my way into the sunlight and head for the Palace of the Popes or for the funicular railway up an Alp. When had I ever had this much fun at old Forbes Field?

Of course, it wasn't *always* pleasant. Especially in France. I had composed a long letter in English about my search for Wilkes manuscripts and had sent it to the Archives Nationales in Paris. There was no response, but when I was ushered into the office of the archivist in charge of *manuscrits étrangères*, I saw my letter open on her desk. In *her* language she launched into a rapid explanation of what finding aids I might wish to examine, what *fonds* I should explore, and, for all I know, the condition of the roads between Paris and Avignon. I nodded my head agreeably at what I took to be appropriate inflections, muttered a comprehending "d'accord" at key intervals, here a "oui," there a "oui," everywhere a "merci beaucoup."

I think the French do it to everyone.

The English seem to be a bit more relaxed—about their books and their language.

The most congenial library among my souvenirs is near Chester in the northwest of England. It is St. Deiniol's, a residential library at Hawarden (pronounced "Harden," of course) run by the Anglican Church and specializing in works about, and in the collections of William Ewart Gladstone, Prime Minister of Her Majesty, Queen Victoria.

Before I visited St. Deiniol's, I thought a residential library was a place like the Huntington or the Newberry where scholars congregated from afar and resided in the vicinity for a few weeks or months while pursuing their research. But at St. Deiniol's scholars and free-lance writers came to live, eat, and study. Relatively Spartan bedrooms upstairs were fitted out with desks and chairs, washbasins, and metered electric heating; the library downstairs was comfortable, large but not massive. The atmosphere encouraged a leisurely bibliophilic approach to reading and writing.

I would have stayed longer—the peace and pace agreed with me. I even took a modicum of interest in the late afternoon croquet matches on the green back lawn. As Eliza might have said, it was the food what done me in. Each meal was preceded by a formal grace spoken by the Warden, a collared cleric of the Anglican Church. After this blessing, the assembled residents settled down to the plates of food on the table. Quantity was not the problem. My first dinner consisted of sole, mashed potatoes, and cauliflower, accompanied by white bread. The second meal presented some pale veal snuggled up to a few turnips and boiled potatoes. White fish (unidentified), rice, and cauliflower in a cheese sauce composed the third meal. There was lovely rice pudding for afters again. I had never thought it possible to be willing to kill for something green—a bean or a spear of broccoli. When the Warden had blessed the fourth meal, consisting of macaroni and cheese plus the softly yielding white bread, I excused myself and searched out the Fox and Grapes at the end of the road. A pint of lager, a ploughman's lunch—lettuce, tomatoes, cucumbers, along with cheeses—eased the pain. In the dark recesses of the smoky room I thought I spotted a few fellow denizens of St. Deiniol's, but we looked away like fellow deacons caught in a burlesque house.

Realizing that my interest in the croquet game probably had more to do with the greenness of the grass than the sport itself, I knew it was time to bid farewell to cozy old St. Deiniol's. Even Queen Victoria could take Mr. Gladstone only in small quantities.

While St. Deiniol's was quite special, every library has its own quality, created more often by the guardians of the treasure than by the dispensers of the food. Sometimes, as in the magical Duke Humfrey reading room of the Bodleian at Oxford, the physical setting—the desks with shuttered bookshelves above them, the old wood, the staircases—produces the unique flavor. Usually, however, the ambience reflects the rules and regulations and the librarians or archivists who enforce them.

In some places there are stone gargoyles protecting the books against the users; other libraries are Liberty Halls. The most casual I have encountered is Chetham's in Manchester. It is really Chetham's Hospital, once upon a time a school, and still housed in a fifteenth-century building with marvelous dark corridors, low stone archways, and wide stone staircases. Today it is a music conservatory as well as a library, and the soft sounds of choral music or a small chamber group waft through the windows as you are leafing through rare volumes or searching for a title you want brought to you.

While most libraries have heavy wooden cabinets filled with drawer after drawer of cards containing all the details about the books or manuscripts in the collections, Chetham's has—or had back in 1970—a unique system. Looking for materials on voyages and travels as well as anything on John Wilkes, I arrived in Manchester one autumn afternoon and ducked my head to pass through arches never intended for six-footers. I found my way to the librarian in charge. She led me through another series of dark, winding corridors to a table by an open window and presented me with an eight-inch stack of flimsy slips of thin paper all held together precariously by a worn rubber band.

"This," she said, "is our card catalogue for travel literature. The slips are in alphabetical order, and if you go through them, you ought to be able to find out whether or not we have what you are looking for."

Then she left me to my studies. Unfortunately, as soon as I removed the rubber band, it snapped. Simultaneously, a breeze sprang up outside, and a few dozen slips of paper from the card catalogue flew, free at last, around my little work space. I corraled as many as I could, stuffed them back into alphabetical order— more or less—and covered them with a nearby reference book. For about an hour I flirted with disaster, lifting the volume, riffling through the slips, protecting the fragile things against sudden drafts, and felt myself fraying like the rubber band. I kept imagining a gust coming up (the window proved impossible to close), and the entire listings of travel literature in Chetham's Library fluttering around the high-ceilinged room like so many errant paper airplanes.

When I finally handed the stack back to the librarian and asked for a few books I wanted to see, I felt tremendous relief. The books themselves, old and rare, were delivered to me in another solitary recess, far from the librarian's abode. For an hour I was left by myself to sort through half a dozen of Chetham's treasures, with other similar gems shelved all around me.

Such freedom was almost too much for a scholar accustomed to the more stringent policies of university libraries' special collections. One I often visit is housed in an imposing structure wherein the precious books lie in splendor, and generally in solitude. *If* a prospective reader makes it past the front desk and into the room where books will be delivered, he or she receives a triangular wooden block on which a capital letter appears. Setting this block on your table will enable a page to deliver the book to the right place. Since I have hardly ever seen another reader at any of the other twenty-three tables in the room, I have occasionally, albeit timidly, questioned this practice.

"It is the rule," I am told.

All the tables are equipped with folding reading stands and felt-covered sandbags for holding the books open. And all the tables and stands are set up to face away from the door and away from a glassed-in area where a librarian comes to observe whenever a reader accidentally finds his way in. One never knows, I suppose, what desecrations lurk in the warped minds of rare-book readers. For reasons which probably have to do with an insecure childhood, I hate to have my back to anyone when I am working. I do not know whether I fear an attack by a rabid librarian or what, but I sometimes turn the reading stand around and sit facing the observation booth, the volume inaccessible to the eyes of the watchers. Such a move brings a librarian or student assistant promptly to my table.

"The stands are supposed to face the other way."

"Why?"

"They just are."

My assurances that I will not scribble notes in the margins, lean on the fragile bindings, or draw mustaches or obscene appendages on the occasional portraits have no effect. It is even worse when I have the temerity to remove the volume from the reading stand and hold it in my hand while I turn the pages.

A librarian is there in seconds. "You must use the reading stand and a sandbag to hold the book open."

"Why?"

"It is the rule."

On my more feisty days I try to reason with the functionary dispatched to correct my gross abuses. "It is easier on the old books," I begin soothingly, "if they are cradled gently in the hand, their delicate spines supported like a baby's back, their bindings never cracked by being opened too far or pressed too heavily by a weighty sandbag."

Patiently the librarian listens to my rationale. "Well," comes the inevitable response, "that's all right for you because you are a professor of literature and know how to handle the books. But what if the others in the room—students, or professors of business—see you doing that? They'll think they can do it too. What if everyone treated the books that way?"

I look around at the twenty-three empty tables, their reading stands like good little soldiers all facing the same direction; I peer hard to see if perhaps I have missed some dwarf reader hidden behind or beneath a folio text. But I have not. There is nobody else in the room. I point this fact out.

"No, not today," the librarian says, "but there might well be tomorrow." Scarlet O'Hara could not have put it better.

The only library where I have been watched more closely is the Victoria and Albert in London. Known more for its museum than for its books, the V&A had a rare copy of John Wilkes's obscene parody of Pope's *Essay on Man*, the one a disapproving copy machine operator had refused to duplicate for me. When I asked for the poem at the V&A, I was informed that I would have to read it under the direct supervision of a librarian. The fear was not, apparently, that I would deface their copy but rather that I might read it and react in some lewd, lascivious manner detrimental to the public welfare. Have you ever read pornography while being scrutinized by a public servant? I struggled to keep my facial expression immobile, fighting back the occasional leer which sprang unbidden to the corners of my mouth. I took notes halfheartedly, afraid the tight-lipped gentleman staring unsympathetically at me might think I was copying out some of the juicier lines.

With experiences like these, how could I help being nervous in the *laissez-faire* atmosphere of Chetham's Library? Most of the time, however, the policies and the ambience of a research library strike a compromise somewhere between these extremes.

Take the Palaeography Room at the University of London. Wading through many of the 17,000 items in their shorthand collection, I spent a great deal of time hunched over the same table (facing the door, I might add) throughout most of a sabbatical year. I grew to be a part of the furnishings, generally disregarded by the librarians once they had brought me my daily fix of brachygraphical tracts. They did not fear that I would rip out sample pages or begin my autobiography on the flyleaves or in the margins. I was allowed to fondle the books in my hot hands, tickling their ribbed spines to my heart's content.

A few months into my sojourn in the Palaeography Room, I saw a new reader with three or four large folio volumes in front of her, one of them propped on a reading stand. As a regular I could spot a newcomer almost as quickly as members of the staff could. I was struck not so much by her long, straggly, jet-black hair or her granny gown and tattered cardigan as I was by the fact that she was chewing gum. Not so much by the actual fact of her chewing but rather by the manner of it.

Absentmindedly, as she pored over the folio pages, she reached to her mouth and the wad of gum. Slowly, distractedly, she would pinch the gum and stretch it out to a long thin strand and then return it. She was unaware, I was fascinated. And appalled. This behavior continued for the next few days while she chewed her way through more of the old folios. What I could not understand was why the librarians who ignored only harmless duffers like me had not had a "See here now" chat with their new reader. (The English are born knowing how to do this.) Yet there she sat, turning the pages with those long-nailed fingers which only recently. . . . Never mind.

Unable to stand it any longer (maybe I was not so different after all from the book police behind the glassed-in window), I described to one of the librarians what I had observed.

"Oh, yes, we know," she answered.

"You know? But why hasn't anyone said anything to her?"

"Oh, we have. More than once."

I was dumbfounded. How could you allow a gum-stretching reader to turn the pages of rare volumes?

A few days later the reader left, and the mystery was cleared up.

"It was the books," my librarian friend explained. "Did you see what the topic was?"

I had not.

"Witchcraft," she said. "All the volumes were on witchcraft. And she was copying down the incantations. None of us wanted to make her angry. You can never tell with readers, you know."

I knew.

The great London library which has had its share of odd readers is located within a hundred yards of the University of London. After all those years of looking forward to this staple of library collectors, I finally made it to the British Museum, or the British Library, as they now call it to distinguish the books from the mummies. The beautiful blue-domed reading room with its spokes of tables and chairs coming away from the central information desk and circle of bound volumes cataloguing the holdings is a must item for any dedicated collector. An aura of high seriousness permeates the room. (There is a wonderful story—possibly apocryphal—about a puckish guide encouraging tourists to "try the famous echo in the Reading Room of the British Museum." Absorbed and frail scholars gathered from all over the world would drop like flies from the shock.) What visitors always look for is the numbered place at which Karl Marx spent so many afternoons researching and writing *Das Kapital.*

Unlike the easily accessible reading rooms at the New York Public Library, those at the British Library are restricted to scholars who present credentials as well as cogent reasons for working in this particular library. But enough characters do manage to slip

through the net that it is always worthwhile to do as I do and peek surreptitiously at whatever the person in the next seat is reading or writing. Most of the time it is just like my own work, and I go back to my books, yellow pad, and note cards.

One day, however, I glanced over at the middle-aged, bespectacled gentleman beside me. He was copying material from a book onto a yellow lined pad. Just like me. But the heading on his pad caught my eye: "Chapter 7," it read. And then a title: "Seminal Juices: The Last of the Great Treacles." Although I edged my chair a bit further away (the woman on my left gave me a quick, nervous glance), I must admit that my eyeballs were riveted to his page. Unfortunately, I could not decipher any of the tiny scribblings below the chapter heading, and we never got to Chapter 8.

For the past few years, ever since that startling glimpse of work in progress, I have been scouring new-book lists and pulling odd volumes off the shelves in a few bizarre bookstores—mostly in the Times Square area—but without success. Of course, I do not know whether I am looking for a *Joy of Something* manual or a piece of postmodern fiction, but I know I would recognize it if I could just take a quick look at Chapter 7.

Generally, however, the scholarly life at the British Library is not nearly so arousing. Readers lucky enough to find a seat look up desired titles in the bound volumes, fill out a call slip with details like author, title, shelf mark, and their seat number or an indication that the book should be brought to the North Library, the usual watering hole for eighteenth-century scholars working with rare books. Depending on the number of requests, books are usually delivered in an hour or two, occasionally—if the book is housed outside of London at the Woolwich repository—in a day or two. Once in a while, a reader will learn that a book is unavailable.

On the back of the British Library call slips are a number of standard reasons for "non-delivery." "In Use" is, of course, the most common explanation. But one set of possible difficulties has a peculiarly British flavor:

> At Binders
> At Labellers
> At Furbishers

I have never been told that one of my books was at the furbishers. But it has such a lovely ring to it: "I cannot complete my research because a key text is being furbished."

"Have you quite finished with this volume, sir?"

"Yes, for the time being. Please furbish it and return it to me next week."

"Very good, sir. Will that be all?"

There is another set of explanations for non-delivery which is even more intriguing:

> It is regretted that:
> —this work was destroyed by bombing in
>   the war; we have not been able to
>   acquire a replacement
> —this work has been mislaid
> —this work has been missing since:

"Mislaid" conveys such a wonderful sense of imminent discovery while "missing since: 1962," or whatever, rather discourages all but the most optimistic.

Very rarely, none of the printed categories will do, and the disappointed researcher finds a check in the box which reads: "For further information please apply to Book Delivery Enquiries, or Enquiry Desk." My request for a seventeenth-century travel book once brought me to the Enquiry Desk. The volume had not been

destroyed by bombing, it had not been mislaid, nor was it enjoying a quiet fortnight at the binders, the labellers, or the furbishers. It was in a locked case.

"Why can't you simply unlock the case and remove the book?" I asked in my most reasonable tone. We Americans are a practical lot.

"We are sorry, sir," the attendant answered, "but the key has been mislaid, and the locksmith is on holiday this week."

At least the book was safe and accounted for.

The only other time I was referred to the Enquiry Desk was a result of a call slip on which both "destroyed by bombing" *and* "please apply" at desk were checked. Actually, "destroyed by bombing" had an equivocal squiggle inked in after it. Somewhat perplexed, I reported to the appropriate window.

"Ah, yes," said the librarian in charge, looking at his own copy of the non-delivery slip. "This book is in an unsafe area." He laid down the last phrase as if it would make everything quite clear. It did not.

"I don't understand."

"The bombing," he explained. "It weakened some areas of the

building structurally. The volume you want is, unfortunately, inaccessible."

I suppose the American "can do" spirit was evident on my face despite the layer of English discretion I had acquired during the year in London. He went on to dispel my unspoken criticism: "We cannot ask our assistants to fetch volumes which are in an 'unsafe' area. It is too dangerous."

Desperate for the book, I offered to fetch it myself. This brash proposal quite disturbed the librarian.

"We cannot allow that, sir. How would it look if a reader were to fall through the ceiling?"

What he meant, I suspect, was that there was no appropriate place on the B.L. accident form to report a reader lost in an "unsafe" area. I did not pursue the topic further. The Bodleian probably had a safe copy.

I discovered a rather different kind of "unsafe" library when I again crossed the Channel in search of letters. Before departing London, I had searched the various bibliographic finding aids for manuscript letters on the Continent and had been able to concoct the delightful scholarly trip to Grenoble, Besançon, and Avignon. Away from the pleasures of southern France, however, there were still a few extant letters in small, remote libraries I could add to my collection. One of these was the Bibliothèque Municipale in the city of Nantes, a two-hour train ride from Paris.

Armed with details on two letters by Wilkes and notes on twenty-five other letters by his French acquaintances, some of whom might refer to him, I arrived in Nantes about two P.M. on a Thursday. Unless I could wrap up my business expeditiously, I would spend the night there. I went straight from the train station to the library, carrying my small suitcase with me.

The information copied down in London proved accurate, and a diminutive, balding, and very precise librarian who did not, or would not, speak English went off to fetch the two Wilkes letters. Almost ten minutes elapsed before he returned, prompt service in any research library. Unlike the format used for large collections at the Clements or the British Library's Manuscript Reading Room, with letters lightly pasted into bound volumes, here the letters were loose single sheets of paper. It made little difference to me at the time because I spent the remainder of the afternoon contentedly copying out by hand transcripts of the two letters. I did notice a stipulation limiting a reader to no more than two items at a time, but I foresaw no difficulties. It would have been easier if all of my twenty-five references were in a single volume of tipped-in letters, but how long could it take me under any circumstances?

I spent the night in a small hotel and returned early in the morning to the Bibliothèque Municipale. I planned to examine the twenty-five letters containing possible references to Wilkes and catch the noon train back to Paris.

My balding librarian of the previous day smiled in recognition as I came up to his desk to request the first two items. He returned ten minutes later and laid them on the table for me. Whereas the day before I had been content to scribble away with my two letters for an entire afternoon, today I needed only a few minutes to perceive that neither of these missives referred to Wilkes. I might as well go on to the rest. I tried to hand in half a dozen slips, but the little librarian smiled and shook his finger at me, a gentle reminder of the ground rules for manuscripts.

I went through the next two letters as quickly as I had done the first pair. I returned them to the front desk and handed him two more slips for two more letters. He pursed his lips and was about to say something but changed his mind. Off he went to fetch the two requests. Each trip was taking approximately ten minutes— five minutes to the vault and five minutes back, I presumed.

When I laid down my ninth and tenth slips, the explosion came. He waved those pieces of paper in the air with one hand, gesticulated wildly with the other, and proceeded to excoriate me roundly (here the tone was most helpful to a lagging translator) in rapid and very idiomatic French. Even Speed-Listening 890 in graduate school would not have covered all the details. But I think I got the thrust of it. I attempted in measured eighteenth-century French (my entrée to the language) to convey my sympathy and to suggest to him that if I might have all the letters at once, I could save him "beaucoup de travail."

"C'est impossible!"

Aided by a few imaginative pantomimes, I explained that I would be going back to Paris on the noon train. (Shades of Thurber's classmates keeping Bolenciecwcz eligible for the Illinois game—"Choo-choo-choo" and "Chuffa, chuffa, chuffa.") At the news of my imminent departure, the choleric librarian brightened visibly. With a dismissive Gallic shrug of the shoulders, he gathered all my remaining call slips and returned in ten minutes with a dozen or so manuscript letters. To my "merci beaucoup," he nodded curtly. I completed my research in a nervous half hour, gathered up my notes, suitcase, and raincoat, and offered him a friendly "au revoir" as I headed for the door.

"Non, monsieur," he said. "Goodbye."

I reached the station well before high noon, the hour I had promised to leave Nantes, and caught the Paris train with time to spare.

I suppose every collector has a special item or two, a rarity amid the mundane. When I collected baseball parks, I was always partial to a tiny one—in Sherbrooke, Quebec, yet—which, as a minor-league park, was not even in the collection proper. For all the antique charm of the Bodleian, the natural setting of the Huntington, or the medieval surroundings of Chetham's, the Bibliothèque Municipale in Nantes will always be special to me.

I've been offered two Newberrys, a Folger, and even a Kongelige Bibliotek in Copenhagen for it. But I'm not trading. How many scholars have been shown manuscripts only on the condition that they leave town on the noon train?

PROFESSORIAL BUSINESS

THE UNIVERSITY OF ———— REQUESTS
THE HONOR OF YOUR PRESENCE

M any an aspiring academic has been traumatized by the search for that first full-time position—the scores of letters of application, the plumped-up résumés, the rejection letters, the interviews at professional meetings ("The Flesh Market"). With interviews set up by letters and phone calls the ABD's (All But Dissertation) converge on the convention hotel prepared to dazzle prospective employers and to obscure the fact that only the prospectus for the dissertation has actually been written.

Even now, I remember vividly the events of that first job search and my first academic convention. The Modern Language Association meetings, always held in a three- or four-day period after Christmas, were in Chicago that year. Despite the fact that my wife was nine months, and a little bit more, pregnant, I had arranged a dozen job interviews at MLA, and I had to drive up with some other Ph.D. candidates from Bloomington, Indiana. Four of us were sharing a room at the Palmer House. (Convention hotels have always seemed very humane to me, looking elsewhere while four, five, eight job seekers cram themselves into double, and even single, rooms.) Just before dawn on the twenty-eighth of December the phone rang in our Palmer House barracks. The man who had drawn the shortest straw in the previous night's lottery was curled up on the floor by the telephone.

"It's for you," he muttered in my direction.

I left the warm bed (a lucky draw), stumbled across another loser huddled on the floor, and made my way to the phone. The marriage almost came unraveled right then. It was my wife on the phone. She had just been delivered of our second daughter and wanted, she chirped, "to let you know right away."

I cringe even now as I recall my sleepy response. Mumbling

something like "That's fine" or, worse, "That's nice," I hung up on her. My three roommates have never let me forget that phone call. Nor has my wife. It took one very long conversation later in the day to explain things to her. But that daughter, ignored on her entrance to the world, has hardly ever had a father at home for her birthday.

The long day which began in this peculiar fashion ended when I had my interview with the University of ———————, a meeting which had been arranged in a curious way. Normally, the applicant sends out a batch of letters to possible employers and waits for responses which may suggest a meeting at the MLA convention. The interested department asks if a given time and date will be agreeable. The lucky candidate might—at least in those days— set up a dozen or more interviews although there might be a few quick notes or even a phone call or two before mutually accept-able times and dates for interviews could be worked out.

Among the responses I received to my letters of application were a fair number of polite demurrers, ten or twelve letters setting up tentative interview times—and one form post card. This card, a model of efficiency, came from the English Department of one of our great middle western megaversities. In answer to my de-tailed letter and accompanying résumé, the card was succinct yet adaptable. Most of it was typed, but there were a few blank spaces in which somebody had inscribed the pertinent details:

Dear ——————:

Thank you for your application. We have set up the follow-ing interview for you at MLA:

Place ——————

Date ——————

Time ——————

We look forward to meeting you.

Yours truly,

[Chairman's name stamped in]

I examined the card carefully to see if there were any other messages scrawled in out-of-the-way locations, but how many hiding places can there be on a post card? I looked again at the appointed time for the interview and realized that it was impossible: I had already agreed to an interview at that hour.

Consequently, I wrote a pleasant little note to the Chairman, explaining my problem and indicating a range of free hours on a different day. I expected a little note in return. What I received was another of the form post cards with a new date and time written in—and that was it. Improbable as it may sound, I had in the interim agreed to talk to representatives of another university at the precise time inscribed on the second post card. I sighed, and wrote once more to the University of —————, apologizing for this additional complication and suggesting a new time for our meeting. A few days before I was scheduled to leave for Chicago there arrived the now-expected third post card with the date and time I had indicated. Not a morsel more! I have to admit I was somewhat miffed, but I suppressed my irritation. Job-seeking graduate students can afford many emotions—joy, sadness, confusion, anguish—but not irritation at a department rumored to be hiring *two* assistant professors. I wrote the time and date carefully in my little black appointment book, purchased expressly for my first MLA.

At 8 P.M. on the evening of my daughter's birth, after a very long day of interviews, I knocked on the door of the University of ————— in the Palmer House. I was rather nervous about the likelihood of meeting the Chairman, a man with a reputation for feistiness and occasional fierceness. The Chairman himself—not a rubber stamp as far as I could tell—appeared at the door and invited me in. He conducted the interview himself and, except for his request that I sketch for him my "theory of composition," it was all quite civilized. (Under ordinary circumstances I would have had trouble producing such a theory: after a 6 A.M. phone call and ten job interviews I doubt that I could have defined a sentence.) When I left, I knew I was not going to be offered a job at the University of —————.

During bleak January some prospects turned warm, others cooled. I visited Lawrence, Kansas, and stayed at the historic downtown hotel ("Welcome Quantrill's Raiders!" "Try our Soup and Salad Bar!"). On a morning when the bank thermometer outside my hotel window registered five degrees below zero, I was offered a job. I was still shivering when I returned to Bloomington, but the new baby had to be paid for, so I wrote to Kansas and accepted the position. After the excitement of December and January, February dragged a bit, and I filled the gaps in my dissertation writing by sending letters to English departments which had interviewed me. I thanked them for their time and withdrew my name from further consideration. I spent a few minutes mulling over the post cards from the University of ——————.

Of course, I should have known better, but who could resist?

Digging down into the drawers and cubbyholes of my desk, I finally located an old blank penny post card. (I hadn't *seen* a penny post card in fifteen years.) It was dog-eared and generally battered but perfect for my purposes. I slipped it into the typewriter and set up my own form:

Dear ——————:

Thank you for your time at our recent interview. However, I should like you to remove my name from consideration at ——————. I have just accepted a position at ——————. I look forward to seeing you next year when MLA meets in ——————.

Yours truly,

————————

With my fountain pen I filled in the blanks—the University of Kansas for my new employer, Washington, D.C., for the next MLA, and my own name.

Over the next few weeks I scribbled industriously on my dissertation (I was a little embarrassed by the wild promises about finishing it I recalled tossing off in Kansas) and forgot my correspondence with the University of —————. But one day there arrived in my mailbox an official-looking envelope, with the Chairman's name written in the upper left-hand corner. Despite all my smart-aleck high spirits about getting my first job, I now felt some very distinct qualms. I was not at all clear about what the consequences might be for insulting the chairman—this particular Chairman—at a powerful department of English. I began to wish devoutly that I had let well enough alone. With uncustomary trepidation I opened the envelope. "At least," I thought, "they do not have a form post card for this one." At the moment I did not feel like celebrating my small victory. The letter floored me. It was a hand-written, cordial, gracious, pleasant acknowledgment of my news (without any reference to my postal medium), warm congratulations on my choice of employer, and sincere good wishes for my future success in The Profession. And it was signed by the Chairman.

Even as a callow youth, a rank amateur in the arbors of academe, I could recognize genius, and I knew I had just been demolished by a master of one-upmanship. I stopped writing post cards.

And, for penance, I took to whistling "Hail to the Victors."

ACADEMIC CONVENTIONS

There are certain academic conventions. I mean beyond tenure and chatting up the dean at a dinner party.

Scientists, humanists, administrators, eighteenth-century specialists, in groups large and small, go off to meetings once a year—in cities like Chicago, Los Angeles, Atlanta, New York, and New Orleans, to name a few. What goes on at these conventions is very much like what I imagine goes on at gatherings of pharmacists, insurance agents, or cement contractors. The Shriners, I understand, are different. There are a couple of days set aside for lectures and reading aloud of papers, some artistic performances, and a few formal banquets.

For the twenty-five years or so since that first interview-crammed MLA, I have been attending such meetings—the MLA, the American Society for Eighteenth-Century Studies, the Northeast American Society for Eighteenth-Century Studies (the acronym NEASECS is pronounced KNEE-SEX; four patella fetishists showed up by accident one year), the Johnson Society, and others.

After abandoning my family in late December every year for fifteen years to attend the MLA convention, I finally lapsed and skipped one in Chicago. I had preregistered, sent in money, reserved a room at the convention hotel, and booked an airline flight. But on the 23d of December, snow swirling in Kansas and in Chicago, the fireside began to look better than hearing a paper on Gray's *Elegy* Revisited or The Right Whale in *Moby Dick*. Aware that I would lose my ten-dollar convention deposit, I called and canceled my reservation anyway. Hotel, airline, MLA, the works.

It felt so good after Christmas *not* to be going to MLA in frigid Chicago, that I began to speculate on the pleasures of not going to conventions—to *plan* to go and then not to go. In order to get the full benefits of not going, one ought to register and reserve space—to feel the pressures mounting, to pull out that old suitcase—before canceling. Then I realized that there are some cities it would be more satisfying not to be going to than others. What if one could set up an organization—say, Conventions Anonymous—which would arrange for individuals to commit themselves to attending conventions in places like Harrisburg, Fort Wayne, Little Rock, Davenport—the list seemed endless. For a small nonrefundable fee we would send out programs, city maps, and brochures of area highlights (some of those places would require real creativity). Then, a few days before our subscribers were to leave home, they could write to us, canceling, or—a variation—we'd write to them, informing them that, alas, the convention had been called off—a reactor leak in the lobby of the convention hotel, an outbreak of sleeping sickness among the bellhops, a geological fault newly discovered in downtown Birmingham.

I was never able to get the plan off the ground. The trouble is that when scholars congregate, even if it is in Normal, Illinois, or Columbus, Ohio, they drink and talk and drink some more and stay up late and forget that they are not having a good time.

Like most conventioneers, academics wear name tags. These do not normally read "Hi! I'm Shelby Snell," but rather announce the name and affiliation—thus: "Shelby Snell, Lower Ravine College." Now anyone who has played the Name Tag Game for any length of time knows that one "J. Hillis Miller" is worth ten, maybe twelve, "Shelby Snells." Hence, the rules of this academic Pac Man: do not look at faces or shapes; look only at name tags. A crowded elevator always contains one or two heavy peerers trying to get a good look at the badges worn by the others going up or down with them. Most of the time the collector won't do anything when he spots a "Harold Bloom" or a "Helen Vendler." What stories he will embroider on his return to South Bellingham or West Topeka are, of course, the stuff of local legend. ("Did you hear that Shelby had a long conversation with Walter Jackson Bate at MLA?" Translation: Shelby asked Bate what floor this was, and Bate told him where to get off.) Occasionally, a Shelby-the-Bold will go further: "Ah, Professor Booth, I thought your last book was your best." (This line can hardly lose.)

One of my former graduate-school colleagues is a master at this gambit. And he is unusually adept at following up with explanations of how his own important work (published in the *Ball State University Newsletter* or *North American Notes and Queries*) considers similar problems. I am always glad to see my friend at conventions, and he is always glad to see me. He grips me firmly by the hand, checks my name tag just to be sure he has remembered me correctly (and that I am at the same dull university, holding the same dull job—and therefore not any more important than I have ever been). Then he tracks the passersby as carefully as he can over my left shoulder. He invariably leaves me as I am responding to his interest in what I am working on right now. "Oh, Professor Bowers," I hear him cooing as he moves out of range, "Jean Hagstrum asked me to say hello if. . . ." (I doubt that he knows Jean Hagstrum either, but surely that's beside the point.)

For those who give or listen to papers at scholarly conventions, getting up in the morning is the toughest problem. The poor devils who find themselves reading a carefully crafted paper on the End-Stopped Couplet in Prior's Early Works at 8:30 A.M. on the second morning of a convention know what ALONE means. More often than not, all the *speakers* will make it to the meeting. (I have been to one early morning session where an empty chair went unexplained and implied volumes about the unspeakable debauches of the previous night.) A few local graduate students dragooned by their major professors will be sprinkled about the cavernous hall. Toward ten, remnants of bedraggled scholars begin slinking into the empty seats to await the first coffee break. The only worse time to be scheduled is in the final program of a convention that ends at noon. Reversing the procedure of the early-morning meeting, this one begins with a half dozen souls in the audience (all friends of the speakers), who shortly after eleven begin drifting out one after another "to catch a plane." Papers on The Solitary Hero or *The Enormous Room* go over well in these sessions.

But it is not merely the timing of the sessions which creates difficulties. Time is a problem for the individual speakers. A colleague told me about a paper he heard a few years ago. The speaker had just passed the nineteen-minute mark of his allotted twenty minutes. In mid-sentence, with a conclusion not imminent or even conceivable, he put down his typescript, and leveled with the audience. The previous night in his hotel room, hard at work on a conclusion for his paper, he had been interrupted by convivial friends who had invited him out for a drink.

"I went," he said. And sat down.

More often, however, the question is: "Will this speaker never finish?" I have heard of one seventy-five-minute program at which the first participant took so much time—forty minutes intead of twenty—that the fourth speaker was left at the post. Another remarkable occasion which I, alas, also missed, was described for me by a friend. The speaker, she said, appeared to be writing his talk *as* he delivered it. Striding back and forth across the room, he would stop suddenly and jot down a few points on a yellow legal pad. These insights appeared to please him greatly, and after a moment or two of reflection he would resume his ramble. It must have been exciting—albeit unnerving—to be present at the simultaneous delivery and conception of a scholarly paper.

I wish I had been there for that one. But I did hear something like it. At a recent interdisciplinary meeting a hefty, genial, disheveled gentleman sat at the platform. His tie was loosened, his collar unbuttoned, and he wore no jacket. The first thing he said after the moderator had introduced him and announced his topic was, "That's not really what I'm going to talk about." He had changed the title of his paper. A few studious souls in the audience began to write down the altered title, but he interrupted himself, and they never did get it all. Pacing about the front of the room, his shirt-tail now flapping, a friendly smile on his face, he chatted away on a topic which appeared to bear little resemblance to the one listed in the program. He would interrupt one train of thought, begin another, and then interrupt the interruption. Occasionally his enthusiasm led him to tell us, "Now *here's* a good part coming up!" He was enjoying himself immensely, and there was a kind of endearing quality about the whole performance, but a few of the crustier scholars in the audience were frowning deeply. A few stood up and walked out. Then a few more. We have all seen members of the audience rush out at the *end* of one scholarly paper and before the beginning of the next. I have never seen the sort of unorganized but massive exodus I was watching here.

After what seemed like hours he stopped in mid-career. He had not reached any conclusive point or developed any line of argument so far as I could tell. Looking at the moderator of the session, he said pleasantly, "I must have run out of time by now." I and everyone else there expected to hear the moderator respond, "Yea, verily! Finito!" In what is the lowest moment I have ever experienced at any convention, any time, anywhere, I heard the chairman answer, "No, you have seven minutes left."

Just at the moment when the idea of ritual murder—first the chairman, then the speaker—must have occurred to every hardy soul still in the room, the speaker blinked a few times, thought about the answer he had received, and then said, "Oh. Well, I think I'll stop here" and sat down.

A less numbed group would have given him a standing ovation.

I should not be harsh about the efforts of well-meaning speakers. I got my own come-uppance a few years ago on a panel concerned with travel literature. I thought the four of us were doing a splendid job: nobody tripped over the lectern, we stayed within our time limits, and most of the audience was awake when we finished.

We were pleased to hear the moderator announce that because of the great interest in the topic, he planned to convene another session on this same subject next year. Then he went on. Whether he meant in some manner to compliment this year's panel but got confused or whether he meant to say what he did, I'll never know. What I do know is how startled all of us panelists were as he concluded with the hope "that next year we can have much better papers."

The audience's thunderous applause was the most ambiguous sound I have ever heard.

I don't mean to suggest that there are no high spots at these conventions. There have been a few wonderful moments. A memorable one occurred about ten years ago at a Modern Language Association meeting in New York City. A panel of distinguished eighteenth-century scholars, including one eminent curmudgeon who still strikes fear into most faint academic hearts, was gathered to read papers and comment on each other's performance. There they all sat on a raised platform in the Georgian Ballroom of the Americana Hotel. More than a hundred and fifty of us in the audience were prepared to hear some interesting tidbits about art and literature in the eighteenth century.

The first speaker must have smoked three cigarettes in the twenty-five minutes he was hacking through his talk on Newspaper Titles in Hogarth's Etchings. The audience perked up when he was followed by a woman in a Nancy-Reagan-Red dress. We listened attentively as she went through her first two pages. She had become so involved in her own performance that she was leaning over the reading stand, holding her paper dangerously close to the ash tray so overworked by the first speaker.

While she continued to yoke physiognomy in art and literature, the audience slowly became aware of wisps of smoke which seemed to originate at the bottom of her last sheet of paper. We watched in rapt fascination as she read on, oblivious to the smoke that was beginning to curl up over the back edge of her essay. Just as a bright orange flame showed over the top and the smoke billowed, the speaker saw it. She shrieked and threw the paper down on the platform. At precisely this moment the old curmudgeon, who had been listening to her argument with visible displeasure, leaped to his feet and began to stamp on the smoldering paper. He trampled it until the fire was out. I thought he ground his heel into it somewhat willfully, but that's just one man's opinion. It was one of those rare spontaneous and symbolic actions.

The speaker recovered her composure well enough to retrieve the charred pages and read slowly through the remainder, pausing occasionally to reconstruct from memory phrases and sentences that had been burned—or trampled—beyond recognition. It was the finest session I have ever attended at MLA.

There are, of course, other convention highlights, but the 1979 Atlanta banquet tops my list. The preliminary program for the meeting of the American Society for Eighteenth-Century Studies included an intriguing invitation. If enough gourmets could be found, and *if* they were willing to plunk down $45, the Chairman of the English Department at Emory University would arrange an eighteenth-century dinner with the head chef at the Omni Hotel and Convention Center. Around the country twenty-five scholarly sybarites rushed to their local credit unions to borrow the necessary fee. The dinner was on.

Most of us spent the day of the banquet fasting. We actually skipped lunch and went to hear convention papers. (Not really recommended on an empty stomach.) When the cocktail hour had passed, we clambered into taxicabs and headed for the Omni. We were in our places, ravenously hungry, by seven o'clock.

The menu itself was dazzling, but we all assumed that we would be offered a nibble of this or a dollop of that:

First Course
Old English Lentil Soup
Puff Pastry with Veal Sweetbreads, Mushrooms & Cream Sauce
Cold Roast Pork, Jellies, Sauces, Vegetables & Relishes
Sole with Caper Sauce, Boiled Herbed Potatoes
Leg of Lamb, Baked Apples & Fresh Mint
Claret—Hock
Breads

Second Course
Smoked Trout
Guinea Fowl & Pheasant,
Red Cabbage, Bread Dumplings
Pear Compote
Roast Beef & Yorkshire Pudding

Dessert Course
Fruit Tarts & Pastries—Fresh Fruit
Cheshire Cheese—Biscuits—Goat Cheese
Coffee—Port—Tea

Well! Most of us were savvy enough to go easy on the lentil soup and the breads and rolls scattered enticingly around the table. But we still assumed that the menu had been padded.

The extent of our miscalculations became clear only when we had mopped up the last of the puff pastry and the mushrooms in cream sauce. New plates appeared, laden with cold roast pork and the promised jellies, sauces, and vegetables. More wine. Even when new full-sized plates were brought on bearing capered sole, and fresh glasses of white wine joined them, we were holding up rather well, offering cultured and literate toasts to our convener's good health.

The evening went on like this. The red wine and the white seemed to blur together like the colors on a fast-swirling barber pole. I remember offering a toast, but I cannot recall the topic or the conclusion to it. One of our most dignified scholars swayed through a very long and very learned toast before subsiding ignominiously beside his guinea fowl. For some reason—there may have been a ground swell of urging, but I rather doubt it—a Past President of the Society began to repeat from memory the rhyming Presidential Address he had delivered a few years earlier. (I *think* it still rhymed.)

Midway through the various courses, those of us who still could waddled arm in arm around the table, the more bloated ones watching enviously. By the time the Roast Beef and Yorkshire Pudding arrived, few of us could do more than make half-hearted sorties upon it. Only our Past President—he of the rhyming couplets—finished it all and asked for a second helping. We had a sudden insight into how ancient societies chose their rulers—Beowulf was stronger than anyone else, Ulysses more clever. And there was *our* leader polishing off his second plate of Roast Beef and Yorkshire Pudding while the rest of us were thinking bicarbonate.

It was after midnight when we reached our hotel: we had been eating for five hours. The next day whenever one Omni Glutton caught the glance of another, a rolling of the eyes or a cautious patting of the stomach signaled the new-forged camaraderie.

A day or two later I was poured onto an airplane for the trip home to Kansas. Even as I sat there on the plane memorizing a few titles of papers from the program (my crafty chairman always asks me if I have heard any good papers), I felt a few mild twinges of pain in my big toe.

After a day at home I found that the toe had become inflamed and swollen. The next mental leap would have occurred to any eighteenth-century specialist—gout! I called my internist's office and asked the nurse if people ever had the gout any more.

"Oh, yes," she said. "Why do you want to know?"

I explained about the throbbing big toe and then gave her a slightly toned-down version of the Great Feast in Atlanta, reading her a few selected entries from my souvenir menu. She went off to consult the doctor.

When she returned to the phone, she said that he was very interested and would see me immediately. Oh, and would I please bring the menu along?

That's what I get, I thought, for having a gourmet internist instead of a G.P. But I limped in clutching my menu with all its incriminating sweetbreads, jellies, and mushrooms in cream sauce. I offered to remove my shoe, but, no, he wanted to go down the menu with me. We discussed the various delicacies. Once in a while, he'd look up and ask, "You did say this was a *scholarly* meeting, didn't you?"

Well, the whole story is anti-climactic. When he finally finished with the Cheshire Cheese, Biscuits, Goat Cheese, *and* the Port, he allowed me to take off my shoe and sock.

"Sorry to disappoint you," he said, "but that's not gout. It's just a simple infection."

I had a feeling as he sliced into the toe that *he* was the one who was disappointed. That epic meal *should* have produced an attack of gout.

The dinner did, however, broaden tremendously my circle of convention acquaintances. Over the years I have been amazed at the three or four hundred people who claim to have been in our company that famous night at the Omni.

THE PH.D. AND THE IRS
INNOCENCE AND EXPERIENCE

I should make it clear at the outset that this is not going to be one of those "How to Beat the IRS at Their Own Game" essays, nor is it going to serve in lieu of those Tax Guides for Professors. Innocence, that's my recommendation. Honesty, candor, and a bit of the wide-eyed approach professors normally do their best to avoid.

When I recollect the halcyon days of the short form—one year I earned $2700 at a parsimonious Detroit advertising agency—I can only sigh. How simple it was then. Now, I depreciate my professional library, deduct subscriptions to scholarly journals, and take deductible research trips to pleasant places like London, Nantes, and Coimbra. If I teach for a semester at Bowling Green in Ohio or Champaign-Urbana, I scour my records for the deductions accruing to one who has to set up a temporary home "away from his permanent place of residence."

These days I find English professors discussing the intricacies of the tax system in the hallways and watering holes of academic gatherings. Who knows? A colleague may have found the soft underbelly of the Internal Revenue Service.

A few years ago a friend assured me he had located just such a weakness. I suppose I should have been a little more suspicious when I considered that his research interest was sexual repression among the Victorians, but I was hoping that such a specialty might provide a key to the inmost thoughts of agents, lawyers, and auditors for the IRS.

My wife and I were on a trip to the east one summer and had stopped off for a visit. Charles entertained us lavishly, but I could not avoid the thought that his apparently idle question to me— "Wasn't Samuel Johnson sexually repressed?"—would probably turn up in his Form 2106, Employee Business Expenses, to justify the evening. Charles had to stop me after a ten-minute monologue on Johnson's sexual problems. It turned out he really wanted to talk about tax deductions.

"Everything can be deducted," Charles said.

"Well," I admitted, "I do plan to deduct those days on this trip when I am working at the Houghton Library at Harvard and the Beinecke at Yale."

"Everything," said Charles. "Gasoline, dinners, lunches, newspapers, dry cleaning, theater tickets, bandaids—everything."

This did not sound right to me, and I told Charles so.

"Come down to the basement," he said. "I want to show you something."

I tried to get him to show me right there in the living room, but he insisted.

"I have to set up my slide projector."

I cringed. "You're not going to show me slides? You know I hate looking at slides."

"Not slides. One slide."

I finally had to go down the basement stairs, protesting all the way that I did not see how one slide could be all that important to the question of travel deductions.

"You'll see," Charles assured me.

When he had at last set up the screen, warmed up the Carousel projector, and sorted through a couple of boxes of slides, Charles began explaining.

"You remember last year when my wife and I took the children to Europe—France, Germany, Switzerland, and all that?"

I remembered very well the Christmas letter that went on *ad nauseam* about that bloody trip.

"All deductible."

"How," I inquired, "could that be?"

"Watch," said Charles, flashing a slide upon the screen.

It was merely a picture of Charles standing in the snow with a large mountain slope behind him. It was the same kind of slide you and I take every year in Colorado or the Adirondacks.

"That picture," he said, "means I can deduct the whole trip."

In my innocence I looked hard at the picture. Nothing. Innocence and stupidity may easily be mistaken for each other.

"The photograph," he explained patiently, "was taken in Germany."

All right, I thought, forget Colorado. "So?"

"Not only in Germany, but in front of a particular mountain."

"Charles," I said, "get on with it. I don't see what any of this has to do with deducting your European junket." Even in the dark, I thought I saw him wince at the word "junket." I was glad.

"Look," he explained ever so carefully. "That is not just any mountain in the background. That is a very special mountain. It is close to Dr. Frankenstein's laboratory." If his pregnant anticipation meant he was waiting for a light bulb to go on over my head, he would be doomed to sit eternally in his darkened basement.

"Charles. . . ."

"I teach nineteenth-century literature, right? I teach Shelley. Mary Shelley wrote *Frankenstein*, and I teach it. I show that slide in my class. Click. Deductible."

Well, I tried to reason with him. We covered ethics, the law, geography even. Charles had written off the entire cost of airline tickets, lodging, food, tourist guides, everything on the ba-

103

The Ph.D. and the IRS

sis of one Kodachrome slide of him posing in front of Dr. Franken-stein's peak. I didn't even know that Dr. Frankenstein had his own peak.

When we climbed back up the stairs, Charles, with all the au-thority he had now assumed for himself, began to lay out my next two weeks of driving up and down the east coast. "Be sure to buy a post card showing the city squares in Savannah," he said. I looked blank, and Charles looked irritated.

"Do I have to do it all for you? You're the eighteenth-century specialist. General Oglethorpe had dinner with Samuel Johnson, didn't he? General Oglethorpe laid out the squares in Savannah."

"Deductible," I offered.

"Right."

Charles quizzed me briefly on my interests—Johnson, of course, British radicals like John Wilkes, the American Revolu-tion. Then he continued with specific recommendations: a slide of the Liberty Bell, a week in Williamsburg, Virginia, a photograph of me standing in front of the "Wilkes" part of the sign on the outskirts of Wilkes-Barre, Pennsylvania. (I think Charles saw this last item as the equivalent of his mountain.)

Actually he laid out a very nice trip for us. Wilkes-Barre wasn't too exciting, but Philadelphia was interesting, Savannah charm-ing, and we loved the week in Williamsburg.

I have, of course, been audited. More than once. I need not detail the panic created by the form letter suggesting that the IRS would like to visit with you. Now I have always tried to be friendly and sociable and can enjoy a visit as well as the next man. But who invites you over for a visit requesting that you bring along all of your Employee Business Expenses, your supporting documents for claiming an office in the home, and all your canceled checks for a year? I mean, *really*. I haven't even opened half the envelopes in which the bank sends back my canceled checks. (Every sum-mer I stop using my check book for a month or so to let it, as the junkies say, dry out. At the end of the month of inactivity, I see what the bank thinks I have and write that amount down under BALANCE.)

The first time the IRS invited us in for a chat, it took two weeks just to locate the records we thought they'd want to discuss. We drew a friendly but efficient agent who called my attention to a rather intriguing (at least he was intrigued by it) accounting procedure I had, in all innocence, developed for dealing with my "professional library."

"You deduct the cost of all these scholarly books."

"That's right," I responded, confident that there certainly couldn't be anything improper in that. They probably start you out with a few harmless questions before they get to the weekends in Rio or fortnights on Barbados. "Is that wrong?" I asked pleasantly.

"Well, no, but you really should be depreciating them."

"I do."

"Yes," he said thoughtfully, "that's what I'm looking at. You deduct them as a professional expense and then you depreciate them?"

Although I had been assiduously pursuing this efficient system for years, it was only now as I heard it put in those bald terms that I had a glimmering of doubt. "Ye-e-s," I answered, "that is what I do." Then instinct took over: "Shouldn't I?"

He seemed more bemused than censorious. "You are really deducting the books twice."

"Hmmm," I responded slowly. "I never realized that before."

Well, we worked out a less enterprising method for this year and the succeeding ones. We discussed a great many other fascinating tax matters, and I picked up a lot of free advice. When I informed him that I would be on sabbatical in England the following year, he was perfectly willing to counsel me on the amount I should list for meals each day.

"Three dollars per diem would be reasonable," he suggested. Now this was 1970, not 1933, and three dollars a day didn't quite sound reasonable to me. But I guessed—rightly it turned out— that I would never see this particular auditor again. I have always wondered, however, if anyone ever turned in that "reasonable" figure.

The trip to England did not create any tax difficulties. We had so little money for that first sabbatical—half pay for a full year—that I came very close to filling out a short form for the first time since my lucrative advertising days.

By my second sabbatical I was wealthier (everything is relative for professors, of course) and more familiar with the required records and receipts. I had been somewhat shaken, though, by the story of a fellow English professor who had recently been audited. He was regaling a bunch of us one evening with the story of his IRS interview. Scrutinizing his travel expenses, the agent had apparently found a questionable item.

"I see, Professor, that you are deducting all your expenses for this trip to England."

"Yes, I am. My field is English literature."

"But," the agent bored in, "this was not your first visit to England."

"Of course not."

"Then why," the agent asked triumphantly, "did you have to go again?"

My friend told us he knew he was in for a long session.

So when I went over in 1977 for my second trip, I took careful notes on all the new things I had seen. And I kept a meticulous ledger of every expense my wife and I incurred. I listed everything—newspapers, laundry, Cadbury bars, bus tickets—deductible or not, figuring that I could sort things out when tax time came near.

Each evening in London I would return home from the British Library or the Public Record Office and enter the various items in my little ledger, the pounds in one column, the pence in another. When we drove through France on the way to Spain and Portugal, I recorded all the expenses—a copy of *Le Monde*, a crêpe from a street vendor in Paris, a quart of the local red wine from a Super Marché outside Biarritz—in francs. For Spain the entries were in pesetas, for Portugal in escudos. That ledger was a work of art.

Ah, I almost forgot. The purpose of the research/vacation trip through France and Spain and Portugal (you can see how much I had learned since the day when Charles had to spell it out for me) was to visit a parish priest in a dusty village in northern Portugal. This scholarly soul had located a manuscript long thought to be lost and had edited it in Portuguese. I was editing an English trans-lation by Samuel Johnson which had its origin in the long-lost manuscript. I guessed that my only problem with the IRS would be explaining why I had to drive for two and a half weeks in order to get there. When I received my Bring-All-Your-Records invitation, I was prepared with detailed Michelin maps of France and the Iberian peninsula. (The two and a half weeks might take some explaining, but European geography was certainly on my side. You can't drive straight to Lisbon from London.)

On the appointed day, we motored over to Topeka lugging our notebooks, ledgers, maps of Europe, and receipts from hotels, bed and breakfast establishments, pensions, posadas, and pousadas. We were loaded.

The pleasant and very young agent we drew did not raise any geographical questions. She did not ask to see receipts from po-sadas *or* pousadas. But she did settle down with that gorgeously detailed and now gorgeously color-coded ledger. When I made out my income tax, I had marked all the items with different colored inks and crayons, circling here, underlining there until my scrib-bled entries looked as if they were breaking out of a rainbow. I thought she would skim through it, checking a few items at ran-dom. But, no, she read slowly and carefully through every page, every entry for the year. I was impressed and—it is impossible to avoid in such a situation—slightly nervous.

Finally, she put the technicolor ledger down and looked across the table at me. "How," she asked, "did you decide which items to include as deductions and which to exclude?"

It was the moment of truth. All the items I had *in*cluded were marked in purple. I told her so.

"Yes, but why those items and not the others?"

Friends, there are not very many moments in a man's life when he *knows* he's got it made. You can only feel relatively secure as you lay out your full house on the table. The next player might—inconceivable as it is—just might have four sixes. The promotion you have just been given *could*—impossible as it seems—vanish as the company merges with some conglomerate. The moments of imminent victory—and I mean imminent *certain* victory—are rare indeed.

But when she asked "why those items and not the others?" I knew my moment had come.

"Why, that's simple," I said. "If I had any doubt about an item, I left it out. I only put down the ones I was sure about." Although this answer was quite true, it was also undeniably circular.

Well, she looked long and hard at me and glanced one last time at my ledger of many colors. I did not blush then, but I do a little bit now when I think of all the innocence and honesty I was beaming at her. At the time I thought she was marveling at finding such a paragon. Today, I suspect she was thinking that she had never met such a ninny in her life.

But the upshot was that she pushed the book across the desk to me, reluctantly filled out a form to indicate her willingness to let matters stand, and sent us on our way.

And that's why I believe so firmly that innocence, honesty, and candor will carry the day with the IRS. Those, and a 49 cent box of Crayolas. Deductible, of course.

INGENUITY AND THE GRANT APPLICATION

Academics occasionally spend as much time poring over lists of granting agencies and working up attractive research proposals as they do on the research itself. The proposal may be even more creative than the research. Probably all of our universities have workshops in grantsmanship conducted by special assistants who demonstrate how to cut and paste the best parts of various applications together so as to start referees slavering at NIE, NIH, NEH, the Ford Foundation, or the International Center for the Study of Neo-Dermatology. I suspect that the result is a standardized and solid application which does bring in those research-overhead dollars.

That may be fine for the applicant and his or her sticky-fingered university, but what about the committees which are always assembled to scrutinize and evaluate? I have sat on a few of those, and I know that there is a sameness about almost all the applications. Everyone has gone to the same grant-workshop.

But every once in a while a committee will be hooked by a project. Oh, I don't mean that rare moment when we all shout, "Wonderful! This one must be funded." I am referring to the unique communal pleasure when everyone around the table looks up with the shared shock of recognition: we have an original.

Once, on a hybrid committee of scholars from various disciplines, we all came across at the same time a project that would solve the problem of building houses for poor populations in inaccessible areas of the Himalayas. Actually, it might have been the Andes: it was hard to reach. In some fashion that almost none of us on the committee understood, a kind of plaster cast of a house was to be parachuted on to the spot. Then the parachuted frame (providing, I suppose, that it had not landed on the Wicked Witch of the West) was to be sprayed with water and—presto!—SHEL-TER. Doubtless I have been unfair and have left out—or invented—some crucial detail, but the committee just loved that application. If I remember correctly, we voted a new category on the spur of the moment—Approved But Not Funded.

Another time—on a national panel looking at applications for travel grants—one project took the fancy of all five members. It was from a pair of instructors at a small southern college, in Louisiana, I think. It was for a study of music—Danish music. The two applicants were proposing that the foundation send them over to Denmark and support them while they studied Danish vocal music. We began to examine the proposal more carefully. It wasn't just vocal music they wanted to study: it was drinking songs. And then the methodology became clear: what they were proposing was that we send them over to Copenhagen, and they would move from one tavern to another sampling the local music, entering, so to speak, into the *flow* of things. A scholarly pub crawl: we loved it. I believe we were in complete agreement that if there were any funds remaining after our deliberations, we would send them a quart of Aquavit so that they could get started right away in New Orleans or Natchez. The vote was unanimous: five skol to zero.

Actually, getting any committee to agree on applications is not easy. Committees composed of equal dollops of humanist, social scientist, and physical scientist fragment in fascinating ways. I had presumed that it would be the scientists against the humanists, but it wasn't that way at all. The physical scientists, with their massive lists of two-page publications written by five people, were rather snippy about the social scientists, with their much shorter lists of four-page publications written by three people. And, oddly enough, when both groups saw what humanists were getting paid, they were smugly charitable and kept voting us a month's salary as if it were nothing. It almost was. And I think they were amused when, in response to a pro forma question, I would rhapsodize about the value of some project to edit the poems of Matthew Prior or to trace the madness motif in Doris Lessing's fiction. *They* were sorting enzymes, checking temperatures in voles and South American cockroaches, making models of urban voting patterns, and all sorts of other Important Work. (When they

weren't dropping plaster casts on poverty-stricken indigenous populations.)

On panels that consider applications from humanists around the country, the procedures and the responses are a bit different. Here, there seems to be mild agreement about the significance of humanistic projects. Some panels combine scholars and non-scholars, professors and business people. A woman specializing in Charles Dickens may be sitting across from a man editing college texts in the humanities. Sometimes the voting within the committee will reflect the disparate views—A, A, B, A, D. Then the fun begins.

In one group, I remember, we had some difficulty hearing each other as we went around the room recording our preliminary judgments. "A" and "C" were easy enough, but it was hard to distinguish between "B" and "D," so somebody started saying, "B for Boy" or "B, Boy." It was only a short next step to the designation of "D for Dog." I believe it was the vice president of a publishing house who came up with that one, and the way he stretched out "D-o-o-o-g!" and emphasized the vowel implied volumes about his opinion of how he was spending the afternoon. We all picked it up, and I have to admit it was more fun than just plain D.

That was the session which considered my favorite application—even better than the pub-crawling profs. This one looked like a sure winner: it combined folklore, Australian poets, and oral history. The applicant wanted to conduct interviews in Australia with a number of poets, one of whom, we gathered from the application, was quite old and ought to be put on tape as soon as possible. He seemed to be a fairly important poet, although most of us on the panel did not know much about Australian literature.

There was surprising agreement as we went around the table—A,A,A,A. We looked at each other with satisfaction. The only one we had not heard from was a crusty professor whose field was Australian literature, and we knew he would be delighted at our unanimity—and our magnanimity. We waited.

"D," he said. "Dog, Dog, Dog."

We were stunned. A personal quarrel? A proposal poaching on his territory? He did not seem the type to hold a grudge, but you never know with academics.

Each of us offered a few words to support our grade: "Solid credentials and publications for the applicant," "An important study of a neglected area," "A real need especially to get the old poet on tape before it's too late."

At this point our dour specialist broke in. "*If,*" he intoned slowly, "the applicant is planning to conduct a seance, if the applicant has the power to raise the dead, *then* I would be willing to change my D for Dog to an A. The aging poet who seems to have impressed you all has been dead for eleven years. That's D for Dead!"

The silence which followed was broken by a number of chastened "bow-wows" as four humanists, their ears flattened, changed four A's to four D's.

When our Authority left the room for a few minutes, the rest of us sat around discussing whether the scheme to interview the graveyard poet represented ignorance or chicanery. Two of us voted for ignorance; the other two—rather cogently, I thought—held out for chicanery. And *nobody* wanted to ask the old curmudgeon to break the tie.

I guess I have learned a few lessons about applying for grants, the most important of which are: be imaginative, be bold—and be careful. You can never tell when some scholarly Duke of Wellington will be waiting for you just over the next rise.

AFTER-HOURS AMUSEMENT

PARTY TIME IN ACADEME

I have always been intrigued by the fictional versions of the faculty party with its brilliant but brittle conversations, its political maneuvers, and its sly flirtations. I circle about at the ones I get invited to, eavesdropping on dull conversations I could have heard anywhere and fruitlessly looking out for interdepartmental assignations. Then I return to reading the Great Academic Novel of the moment and sadly conclude either that the novelist attends livelier parties than I do (entirely possible) or that poetic license has transformed my good grey world.

Mind you, there have been a few extraordinary evenings over the years.

One came during my first year of full-time teaching when my wife and I decided to take the big step and plan a dinner party. None of your graduate school hamburgers on the grill and a few cans of cold beer. No, sir. This would be a formal, cocktails-before-dinner, sit-down-at-the-table, male-female-male-female, cointreau and cognac afterwards, occasion. We invited my department chairman and his wife plus three of my new colleagues with their spouses. Saturday at seven.

We planned a tasty paella with rice and little shrimps, bits of ham, lots of chicken chunks, green peppers, saffron, the works. I would brandish the cocktail shaker for an hour, and then we would all "go into the other room" for dinner. It was going to be a lovely evening.

The first thing to go wrong was that we were having such a pleasant time at our own party that we forgot about starting dinner itself. I had already distributed two pitchers of cheer, and it was going on for eight fifteen when my wife leaped up and signaled me to follow her out to the kitchen. I thought I would be told to invite the guests to the festive table now laid out with our most matching china and the knives and forks which had spent the least amount of time being ground up by the garbage disposal, our first introduction to the dangers of affluence.

The hostess was near panic. "I forgot to start the paella," she moaned. I peeked into the living room where our guests, well supplied with spirits, were having a perfectly good time without us. We might, I thought, slip out quietly to pick up some egg rolls and moo shu pork or a large combination pizza. But the hostess had recovered her usual *sang-froid*.

"You whip up another pitcher of daiquiris," she instructed, "and I'll light the oven."

"How long?" I asked.

"About an hour, I should think."

My appearance in the living room a few moments later not with an invitation to the table but rather with a fresh, cold pitcher of daiquiris produced a momentary glaze of disappointment and on the face of my chairman a desperate glance at his wife and a barely suppressed whimper. I cheerfully refilled the glasses and opened the subject of The Decline of Literacy, a sure-fire gambit. The guests gamely worried the topic, but I could not help noticing some slurred diction and a few decidedly careless arguments. Certainly not worth more than a B minus.

It took another half pitcher before the welcome sound of "Time to eat" started a stampede to the dinner table. It was nine thirty. With the steaming casserole of paella before me I sat down at the head of the table and began to ladle out generous portions to hopeful guests. New to the role of distributor, I found it difficult to estimate how far the dish would go toward serving ten people. I grew less generous. A measure of incredulity surfaced as the third, fourth, and fifth diners accepted their plates, but they also appeared somewhat resigned. I think they had given up. It did seem to me as I tried to spread grains of rice over most of the plate that the mixture was pretty thin. I tried to give each supplicant some of all the delicious ingredients—some shrimps, some green peppers, some bits of ham. And, of course, some chunks of chicken. It was while I was poking around under the saffron rice looking for chicken that I realized we had another problem. It wasn't that there were very few pieces of chicken: I could have surreptitiously cut those in halves—or thirds. No, there was no chicken at all. In her haste to get the paella into the oven, the hostess had left the neatly deboned chicken sitting on the counter. When her own dainty portion of rice *cum* shrimps reached her at the other end of the table, I saw she was about to remark on my careless distribution of the good things. And then that awful shock of recognition and recollection spread across her face. I thought for a moment she was going to bury her head in her hands right there at her own first dinner party.

The guests had actually perked up a little and were systematically mopping the last grains of rice off their plates. I do believe they were now looking around for a second casserole. My chairman's wife asked if he might have a glass of milk. This request rather surprised me since I had been assiduously keeping his glass topped up with the modestly priced California sauterne (three bottles for five dollars) I had stocked. However, he did look a mite less anxious after he had sipped the milk. The others, realizing the futility of expecting a second casserole, looked enviously toward the milk. At that, I had skipped my own portion of paella, claiming a new diet, but actually having calculated that with two diners left to serve, I might manage to eke out two, but never three, helpings.

Nobody seemed much interested in cointreau or cognac after coffee, and they all left rather early, claiming babysitters who had to be taken home. I thought this odd since all my colleagues were in their fifties and their children in college. In the depressing pillow-talk analysis of the fiasco we decided that they had wanted to get to McDonald's before closing time.

It was not until a few weeks later that we learned the extent of the disaster. One of the survivors who was now inclined to see the humorous side of the evening told us that he thought our chairman had been *in extremis*. "His ulcer, you know." Now it all fell into place—the desperate glances, the whimpering, the glass of milk. The poor man must have looked at that third pitcher of daiquiris, to say nothing of the inexhaustible sauterne, as my personal attempt to finish him off and open the succession to a younger and healthier leader.

As a matter of fact, he resigned the chairmanship at the end of the year. When I heard that he was moving into higher administration in our university, I was worried. He might, after all, hold a grudge. However, when I learned that he was only going to be Dean of the Graduate School, I realized I had nothing to fear. Everyone knows graduate deans are harmless.

I was relieved not to have to see his poor anxious face around the department to remind me of that meatless fiasco. His successor *was* younger and healthier. Unluckily, at my first opportunity— a dinner party, of course—I sat next to his wife, and, in the course of regaling her with a tale of classroom antics, I accidentally tipped a full glass of ice water into her lap. I did not help matters, I suppose, when I tried to blot it up myself, dabbing away at her lap with my napkin.

Such experiences have left me somewhat shy of dinner parties (and other people shy of sitting near me at them). Occasions that mingle students and faculty seem to offer more excitement. For example, one year our undergraduates invited their English professors to a wild affair following the more sedate Honors Banquet. It was far from dull, but it also lacked the subtlety of those fictional parties I had read about. Instead of brittle conversations, political maneuvering, and sly flirtation, there was a lot of loud shouting, dance-floor gyrations, and heavy pawing. As a matter of fact, the mating game got a bit out of hand, and one honors graduate had to barricade herself in a bathroom while her friends pulled a heated admirer away. This was the moment when I decided to leave and was almost sent tumbling down the stairs by the brawlers on the landing. When I did make it out to the street and the night air, I found one of our more contemplative undergraduates considering his empty martini glass.

"Hugh," I asked, as he assisted me gently to my car, "do you students have this much fun all the time?"

"Not really, sir," he said. "Only when we invite the faculty. They seem to enjoy it so much."

I thought about that line the night I attended the one party which came at all close to those fictional versions. One of our most dashing graduate students, who had earlier rented a Chinese restaurant and ordered a special dinner for about half of the English faculty, now decided to give a "Naked Lunch" party in honor of author William Burroughs, who was visiting the campus. I do not recall seeing the guest of honor that night, but then I seem to have missed a number of other sights as well.

We were welcomed at the door by our convivial host bearing a tray of pale drinks he informed us were Fallen Angels. A sensible man would have put the glass right back on the tray after the first sip. It carried an overwhelming taste of mothballs and was, I later learned, a deadly combination of four parts of gin to one part *crème de menthe*.

The action was already lively when we began to move about. Threading my way among animated students and professors clutching their Fallen Angels, I wandered into the room where masses of food, hot and cold, covered a long trestle table. Amid the platters of spiced shrimps, hot cheese rolls, cherry tomatoes, clam dip, and hot meatballs was a long low centerpiece. It took up most of the length of the table.

Sipping warily at my Essence of Mothball, I nibbled my way down the table, maneuvering carefully past what might almost have been called the extended limbs of the centerpiece. About halfway through the Swedish meatballs I became aware that the centerpiece did indeed have arms and legs: it was clad in blue jeans, a white tee shirt, Adidas, and tan socks. It was curled up on its side in a foetal position with its head resting against the bowl of fresh fruit. Inspecting the head more closely, I discovered beneath a glaze like that on a breakfast doughnut the face of a young man. Other guests were picking their way thoughtfully around the display and were discussing the possibility that the centerpiece was actually one of our undergraduate students. The glazed expression seemed to confirm the hypothesis.

By the time I had disposed of my third cheese roll and fourth spiced shrimp, I was positive the centerpiece was breathing. As I

dipped some raw cauliflower into the sour cream, the figure arose carefully from its cluttered bed and wandered off to the toilet. It returned a few minutes later *sans* Adidas and socks. All conversation ceased as it climbed onto the table, curled up comfortably among the hors d'oeuvres, and became comatose. I decided to pass up a fifth shrimp in favor—God help me—of another Fallen Angel. This one seemed to go down more easily, and I could at least assure myself that I was protecting my wool jacket from the inside.

Out of the corner of my good eye (the other was beginning to fog over) I saw the Glazed Man walking past and then, a few moments later, returning to the place of honor, now without tee shirt. The food, which had been disappearing from the table at a rapid rate, seemed to be lasting longer as professors and students alike were growing more timid about reaching for *anything* on that table. I finished my third drink at about the time the centerpiece shed its blue jeans and resumed the foetal position clad only in a pair of flowered briefs.

Even through the haze—internal and external—the symbolism broke through for all us befogged academics—Naked Lunch! The next twenty minutes were going to be crucial. I sloshed into a chair near the trestle table and sipped slowly while I peered intently at the stuffed mushrooms, the avocado dip, and the flowered briefs. A sociable Milton specialist insisted on getting us each another Fallen Angel, singing loudly as he returned of man's first disobedience and the fruit. We awaited the final unveiling.

I blush to admit it, but I never saw the figleaf drop. I understand that it did, but by then I had been poured into the passenger seat of my automobile and unloaded gently on my doorstep. My wife says I got myself to bed, but I recall no details.

What I do remember vividly is just how sick I was. All that night and all the next day I cursed those Fallen Angels with a ferocity that would have made Milton proud. I added a few unkind words for my host as well. When the epic hangover lasted until mid-afternoon *two* days later, I wrote him a curt note indicating my low opinion of a man who would poison his friends—to say nothing of his professors—under the guise of conviviality. I did not mention the glazed centerpiece because I was no longer certain that I had actually seen it.

Later, however, when my head and stomach had returned to their accustomed sizes and functions, and I no longer felt a compelling urge to accept the first offer of euthanasia I could find, I sought out others I thought I could recall at the party. We shared our blurred and somewhat incoherent memories. Evidently, it had all happened pretty much as I remembered. There *had* been a young man couched among the plates of food. He *had* risen occasionally to divest himself of some article of clothing. There *had* been a final revelation—a naked lunch!

In retrospect, now that I was no longer in fear of immediate dissolution, I felt rather proud of having been there. It *was* like those fabulous parties Scott and Zelda used to give. People are always interested when I tell them that I attended the famous Naked Lunch party, and they are fascinated when I describe the periodic disrobing of the glazed figure on the table. In the retelling, I always stay to the end, and what my auditors like best is my detailed description of the shedding of the final garment. I mention the huzzahs, the glasses being smashed, the young man hoisted on shoulders. Envy clouds their faces, and they go away wishing *they* had been privileged to be a part of that wild party scene.

I do believe I have learned how those novelists do it.

RUM RUNNING IN KANSAS

I would like to tell you about one of my earliest adventures in Kansas when I boldly outwitted the law, smuggled contraband liquor across the state line, and raced down the Kansas Turnpike with the aplomb of Burt Reynolds in *Smokey and the Bandit*. I would like to tell you that story. Unfortunately, what actually happened will sound more like Don Knotts in *The Panicky Professor*. Oh, well.

A month after I had earned my Ph.D., I packed my small family into our Volkswagen bus and moved them from Indiana to Kansas to take up my first teaching position. On an early fall evening I found myself at one of those faculty dinner parties where I always listened attentively to my partner on the left and then my partner on the right. I never got much to eat, but my dinner partners were usually quite pleased with me. Tonight I was being regaled by stories of "dry" Kansas and the imaginative methods my fellow scholars employed to purchase spirits across the Missouri line and bring them back to Lawrence. As a newcomer, I found the stories intriguing for what they revealed about my enterprising new colleagues but regarded them merely as party chitchat. I mean, I wasn't taking notes on how to stock my liquor cabinet. (Instructors fresh out of graduate school could not afford liquor cabinets.)

But oddly enough, the very next day I drove the Volkswagen bus, still with its Indiana license plates but sporting a new Kansas Jayhawk parking sticker on the rear window, to Kansas City, Missouri, thirty-five miles away, to purchase a few items for our first house. I found myself parked outside a cut-rate drugstore in downtown Kansas City. What lured me inside was the imaginative window display of bourbon, gin, and scotch bottles instead of the usual—in Indiana, at least—array of shinsplint remedies and new, modish trusses. Wait, if I am going to be truthful in this essay, I had better admit that it was not so much the display itself as it was the rock-bottom prices under the fifths of Old Courthouse, Grampa Boone, and Southern Mulekick. $2.79 for a fifth would have brought any thirsty man on a tight budget in off the streets of Kansas City.

It was all quite spontaneous. "I'll have one of those and one of those and one of those," I announced, pointing at the colorful bottles. When I got back outside to my Volkswagen bus with its jaunty Jayhawk sticker, I had a nice starter collection for my first liquor cabinet. I put the brown paper sack on the floor in the back and drove off.

By the time I had crossed the Missouri River into Kansas, I had completely forgotten my purchases. I was approaching the point where Interstate 70 turns into the Kansas Turnpike, and drivers have to slow down to pick up a turnpike ticket. About a quarter of a mile from the entrance I heard a short burst from a siren behind me, and an unmarked brown sedan pulled up alongside. It was not a police officer, but some kind of badge was being flashed at me. I pulled over to the roadside shoulder.

The man with the badge parked behind me, got out, and walked up to the driver's window. He was dressed in a suit like an ordinary businessman, but he showed me the badge again. FBI or KGB would have been less intimidating. It read Kansas Liquor Authority and brought with it a sudden flood of memory of that incriminating brown sack in the rear. I managed to give him the winsome smile with which we open and friendly Kansas folk always greet each other. I wish he had smiled back. Instead, he said, "You'll have to pull up ahead at the Port of Entry and register this truck."

"Truck?" I repeated stupidly.

"That's right," he assured me. "Up there to the right of the turn-pike booths."

Now although my Volkswagen bus had been called many things—by me and by other drivers—nobody had ever called it a truck. And nobody had ever suggested that I had to register it at a state line. In the brief space of time it took me to move ahead to the Port of Entry and park beside the half dozen interstate semi-trailers, I shuffled madly through all the facts my panicked brain could assemble. This man *knew*. He would not stop me and send me through such formalities if he didn't have *something*. Could I have been spotted in my newly Jayhawked VW outside the drugstore in Missouri? Would the Kansas Liquor Authority do anything so underhanded? (I learned later that the Kansas revenuers did indeed stake out the cheap liquor stores on the other side of the state line, looking for evildoers, but I didn't know it at the time. All I had to go on was terror and instinct—a useful duo.)

I reached the small building labeled Port of Entry. The Liquor Authority agent was waiting for me. "Just come to Kansas?" he asked in what I'm sure he thought was a friendly voice. It scared me to death. I told him that I had been a Kansan for almost a month and that I had been doing a little shopping in Kansas City. He invited me inside.

A number of burly truckers turned to look at me. One of them glanced out the window at my rig. He whistled sharply, and the others looked too. Then they looked at each other and shook their heads. My agent seemed unconcerned.

"All you have to do," he instructed, "is to register at one of these counters." I stood in line.

When my turn came, the Port of Entry clerk took down the details about my "truck" as if he were quite used to such goings on. The question about gross weight drew a few snickers from my fellow truckers. The clerk came to a key entry: was my truck "full" or "empty"?

"Empty, right?" prompted the revenue agent. "Just put down 'empty,' Sam."

As I try to recreate this moment, I am aware of the inadequacy of print. My mind was racing: fears, consequences, escape plans tumbled over one another in rapid succession within seconds before I responded almost immediately. But it takes longer to lay it out here.

When he suggested entering "empty," I thought, "Why?" Why would he say "empty," since if he thought it really *was* empty, he would not have pulled me over in the first place. Surely, he did not really believe that was a truck out there parked among the semi-trailers. What if I responded, "Yes, empty"? Would they smile, wish me "Safe Journey," and send me on my way? Not bloody likely. They would issue me a sticker that read "Empty." I would put it on my windshield, and then the genial agent would say, "Well, let me just take a little look at your empty truck." He would go unerringly to my stash of party supplies, and I'd be up for perjury in addition to whatever else they did to people who were caught rum running.

It was also at this moment in the instantaneous mental dialogue that I recalled one pertinent detail from the amusing dinner table stories of the previous evening. I don't know why I had to think of it now when I had successfully suppressed it so far. Some local entrepreneurs had chipped in $25 to purchase a used jalopy in which to transport their beverages because if you were appre-hended smuggling—such words had taken on a new and painful significance—the authorities would impound your automobile as well as your whiskey. I had a quick vision of a slow walk home along the turnpike to Lawrence. I also thought about the end of my abbreviated academic career: "New KU Instructor Caught in the Act." And after only a month too.

But if I confessed everything right now, then what? Probably the same thing minus the perjury charge.

All of these complicated possibilities were raging simulta-neously through my mind, but I decided almost instantly. Burt Reynolds, you sly dog, move over. When the agent said to Sam, the clerk, "Just put down 'empty,'" I interrupted. "Well," I said, "I did buy some liquor in Kansas City—a bottle of gin, a bottle of scotch, and a bottle of bourbon."

Like those E. F. Hutton commercials, everything stopped in that Port of Entry building. The agent was appalled. He was splutter-ing. "You shouldn't be telling me that!" he gasped. The clerks were all watching the drama, and my fellow truckers were following the conversation with great interest.

"Don't you know," the agent went on, "that is against the law?"

By now I was wholeheartedly into Sincere Innocence, and I looked him straight in the eye when I answered: "Well, I didn't want to say my truck [I thought "rig" might be pushing it a bit at this point] was empty when I had just bought these bottles. I want to be honest about it."

The agent could do nothing but stare at me. My mates of the open road were nudging each other and grinning. I smiled pleasantly at the revenue agent. The clerk had paused at the moment when he had been about to type "empty" into the proper space. An affecting frozen tableau.

Then the agent, shaking his head gently, said, "Just put down 'empty,' then, Sam. But, you know," he said to me, "you really are not supposed to bring liquor across from Missouri. We could impound your car." I noticed he had stopped calling it a truck.

I answered, "No, sir, I won't do that again. I didn't realize it was against the law." (Well, in a way I had simply forgotten the dinner party chat until it was too late.)

They let me go. I had a truck registration form, a gummed square with a huge red E for Empty in the center. I was to stick this to the inside of my windshield and keep it there until I got home.

I felt more like Hester Prynne than Burt Reynolds tooling along the turnpike with my scarlet E blazing away for all to see. My paranoia had not entirely disappeared. Why, I wondered, would the liquor agent hear my ingenuous confession and then still issue me a form indicating that the "truck" was empty. I was being set up. He will suddenly come zooming up from behind, stop me, and search my "empty" truck. He will uncover the detested booze. (For the duration of the trip I was a sworn teetotaller.) He will read me my rights, impound my car, slip the handcuffs on, and take me back to face the smuggling charges *and* the perjury charges.

The twenty-five miles between the Port of Entry and my garage seemed like a hundred. I kept looking in my rear-view mirror all the way home. My heart beat faster as I eased up to the tollbooth at the Lawrence exit. But when the collector accepted my ticket and my dollar without saying, "Just a minute, sir. We have been asked to detain you," I felt a tinge of hope. However, it wasn't until I pulled into my own driveway and my own garage that I felt I had escaped. I shut the garage door, and then I peeled off every last scrap of that incriminating E and made plans for the immediate sale of my Truck.

When I reached the safety of my kitchen, I opened all three bottles and took a long pull at each one in turn. I don't really know why. I believe I thought that if the seals were broken and some of the whiskey gone, then I could not be accused of smuggling. I felt a lot better after I did it.

In the years since my ordeal I have purchased all my beverages from the state-licensed liquor store down at the shopping center. I figure I have spent an extra few hundred dollars in Kansas. But, as I keep repeating to myself on the short, unhurried drive home with those bottles approved and stamped by the Kansas Liquor Authority, you just can't pay enough for peace of mind. I think Burt Reynolds could understand that.

REVENGE OF THE KANJI

A few years ago, for reasons which are now shrouded in the mists, I decided to learn Japanese. I *do* recall how I got myself into the position of even considering the study of Japanese. One day, in a particularly generous mood, I observed my spouse typing away on her doctoral dissertation and gratuitously announced that upon its completion I would take her "anywhere" she wanted to go. I thought she would say "San Francisco" or "Toronto" or some other sensible place. When she immediately piped up with "Tokyo" and "Kyoto," I knew I'd been had.

So instead of choosing a simple subject like molecular biology or astrophysics, there I sat, a middle-aged academic in jacket and tie among the more colorful, and infinitely more casual, freshmen and sophomores enrolled in Japanese I. The students kept darting quizzical glances at me throughout the first period, but the professor, whom I had telephoned about unofficially auditing his course, paid me no special attention. I had wanted to be treated like an ordinary beginner. With the rest of them, I copied out the old chestnut offered on the first day of class—a complete sentence in Japanese. "O, o, o, o, o, o," we all repeated dutifully. We did it again, feeling silly but game. Our professor beamed at us and told us that we had just said in Japanese, "Let's keep our tails covered." Compared to that one, "La plume de ma tante" is a cinch to work into a casual conversation. Still, we left the first class happily chanting it to each other. I taught it to my family, who insisted on using it in our dinner table discussions. My wife, who had gotten me into all of this, reported she had tried it on a Volkswagen Beetle with its rear engine exposed.

For three days a week, when the American professor lectured to us on the sounds and signs of the Japanese language, everything was fine. My fellow students accepted me as no brighter, no duller than themselves. I stumbled through "Arigato gozaimasu" like the rest of them, practiced my "Dozo" and my "ichi, ni, san, shi . . ." aloud with them every Monday, Wednesday, and Friday. But on Kayobi and Mokuyobi I stood out like Mt. Fuji.

On those days our young conversation instructor, a gentle Japanese graduate student named Tsukahama, came, shy and smiling, into the classroom. He was pleasant, earnest, and innately respectful. This last quality applied specifically to me. Because he was the teacher, we appended "sensei"—teacher—to his name. Thus he was "Tsukahama-sensei," and we, as he called the roll, were "Burns-san, Callaway-san, Friedrich-san," and, supposedly, "Gold-san." But he took one look at me among the nineteen-year-olds and froze. Although the professor had told him of the ringer in the classroom, when Tsukahama-sensei witnessed it for himself, instinct and a lifetime of deference took over. So the names were read off: ". . . Callaway-san, Friedrich-san . . . [long long pause] . . . Gold-sensei." My cover was blown.

After class I went up to ask him to call me Gold-san. He smiled in embarrassment: "I will try, Gold-sensei." Well, he did try. Over the next few weeks he struggled manfully. I could hear the tension in his voice, but it always came out "Gold-sensei." I even tried to make out a logical case for him: "In this class," I said, "you are *sensei*. I am student." He smiled appreciatively, bowed slightly, and looked at the floor. My fellow students rather enjoyed the whole "san/sensei" cultural exchange. They took to bowing and calling me Gold-sensei, too.

Not to be falsely modest, I would say that I did rather well for the first few months of Japanese. I sailed through the oral drills with the others. I regularly practiced the writing at home. I learned the fifty-two-character syllabary—the *hiragana* script. Memorized the lot of them. Then, I memorized the fifty-two-character syllabary for words from foreign languages—the *katakana* symbols. Oh, I was some hot tofu, let me tell you. Scratching out those strange little characters on airplanes on my way to conventions of English professors was a surefire means of opening interesting conversations with curious fellow passengers or airline employees. "Is that shorthand?" a svelte stewardess asked in passing. Unfortunately, she could not stay for the full lecture on the complexities of Japanese scripts. Actually, it was that flight on which I came as close as I ever shall to using my complete Japanese sentence functionally. The airline had been advertising their plane as "The Proud Bird with the Golden Tail," and, as we taxied past a flock of them on the runway, I was able to croon happily, "O, o, o, o, o, o."

I even discovered a direct benefit of learning a foreign language. In Boston one evening I was seated at an oval counter in a Benihana of Tokyo restaurant. You know the type: the dinner guests assemble around the counter, and after a suitable period the flamboyant Japanese chef comes out brandishing two very large and shining carving knives, which he flourishes like a high school drum major before bowing to the dazzled and somewhat wary customers. We watched in fascination as he skillfully sliced mushrooms, scallions, and carrots into slivers, all the while grinning and chatting us up in heavily accented English. Then he sauteed some large shrimps with the vegetables on the grill.

When he had finished the cooking, he began to slice the shrimps, pushing a piece at a time to the hungry counter customers. "Ichi," I said for Number One Shrimp, as he shoved the first one towards me. He looked impressed as I counted each time a piece of shrimp came my way: "Ichi, ni, san, shi, go." Each of us had had five shrimps, but there was a sixth left under his sharp blade. "Roku," I said, pointing at the last shrimp. He chuckled and shoved it over to me while the envious monolingual customers had to content themselves with five. After I reported this tangible success to my professor back in Lawrence, I quickly set about learning the numbers up to twenty. You can never tell when you will find yourself at a Japanese clambake where *lobsters* are being served up with the same linguistic favoritism.

This was, I realized later, the zenith of my studies. I practiced my *hiragana* and my *katakana* all the time, often worrying the English Department chairman as I scribbled inscrutable little figures all over sheets of paper while he tried to conduct meetings of the departmental advisory committee. I think he feared it was some sort of code or a cryptic Madame Defarge hit list for after the coup. For my leisure hours I purchased some Japanese records and listened to the music, keeping time with a set of chopsticks purloined from the Boston Benihana.

Then the class was introduced to *kanji*. "These," announced our professor, "are the characters of written Japanese. The *hiragana* and *katakana* symbols you have learned are only modern approximations of the spoken language."

We were suitably attentive. I was suitably stunned. He was now filling the chalkboard with hundreds of ideographs, each of which had half a dozen strokes in it, and every little stroke seemed to have a meaning all its own. He explained that memorizing was the only way to learn *kanji*. Japanese had not originally been a written language: the *kanji* had been brought to Japan by the Chinese.

So night after night, department meeting after department meeting, I struggled to copy out perfect little characters and to memorize their meanings. I began to miss homework assignments for Japanese I. I had to apologize in class or respond with "Wakarimasen"—"I don't understand"—when my turn to recite came around. Tsukahama-sensei was deeply troubled. How could he scold—even gently—Gold-sensei for neglecting his homework? I had less and less time for my assignments while most of the undergraduates, enrolled for credit, were still slogging away faithfully.

One day I raised my hand and asked our professor, "How many *kanji* does the average Japanese know?"

He thought a moment. "About five thousand," he said. "But, of course, an educated person would probably know about nine or ten thousand." I decided it had been a black day in history when the Chinese introduced *kanji* to the Japanese.

Well, my Japan Air Lines calendar languished on the wall. I no longer cared to see what new art treasure might await in November or December. Mozart and Beethoven went back on the stereo, replacing the oriental disks I had purchased only a month before at Takashimaya in New York. I started cutting classes. "Blowing off

class," the sophomores corrected me. I skipped the final examination. I was about four hundred *kanji* behind, and it did not seem a useful exercise. After all, I reasoned, I am only auditing the course.

When the second semester rolled around, and all my young friends were signed up for Japanese II, I found pressing reasons to concentrate on my own teaching and research. My chairman was greatly relieved. So was I. No more *hiragana* or *katakana*. No more *kanji*. *Sayonara*, Tsukahama.

But a final humiliation remained. One day around the Ides of March, when I could remember *sukoshi*—only a little—of all I had learned, when only a few numbers like "ichi, ni, san . . ." and a few odd greetings like "Ohayo gozaimasu" or "Komban wa" could still be retrieved from my fading mental language tapes, I was walking across the campus. I heard a shout from the other side of the street. It was the Chairman of the Department of Oriental Languages and Literatures. Loud enough for every student within fifty yards to turn and stare, he called out, "There he is—

the dropout from Japanese I!" I cringed and began to consider another of my few remaining phrases—*hara kiri*.

That was it for me and Japan. My wife was a fairly good sport about her lost jaunt to the Orient. After a very long weekend during which she played nothing but *The Mikado* and *Madame Butterfly*—at top volume—on the stereo, things settled down to an occasional deep sigh. As for my special Japanese language skills, I have found that a modest reticence is best. Unless, of course, I can cadge an extra piece of fish at the local sushi bar.

TRAVELERS' TALES

WHEELING AND DEALING
AT THE LUXEMBOURG AIRPORT

As the jumbo jets grow bigger so too do the airports. No more the check-in counter and then a brief walk of maybe a city block—two at the most—to reach your flight. If today there should be only a short stroll from counter to flight, woe unto the traveler who is connecting to another airline. "Oh, that would be Terminal B. Take your bags outside and wait for the Red Bus."

Blue buses, green buses, even pink buses will pass by while the traveler keeps checking the time (and possibly scanning the skies) before his plane leaves without him.

Of course, there were problems in the good old more personal days too. I still remember a time back in the fifties when I was trying to fly from Lambert Field in St. Louis to Columbia, Missouri, 130 miles away. One airline had a flight in two hours, but my eye was caught by a small hand-lettered sign indicating that Showme Air flew nonstop (I couldn't help wondering where a plane *would* stop—Moberly? Kingdom City?) between Lambert Field and Columbia. I suppose anyone who had his wits about him would have been warned, if not by the hand-lettered sign, then by the leather-jacketed counter clerk and his response to my inquiry about the time of the next flight.

"Whenever you're ready," he said.

I paused with my money held out in my hand. "But. . . ." He took the money and gave me a handwritten ticket. "Gate 4," he said, "in five minutes."

Dazed, I picked up my small suitcase and headed for Gate 4. There was no attendant so I simply walked through. I was out on the runway. I stopped when I saw just beyond the wire fence a russet-colored (or was it rust?), single-engine airplane with—I swear it—a jagged crack in the front windshield (or whatever they call them in airplanes). But it was too late. The leather-jacketed counter clerk was there, and he picked up my suitcase, took me by the elbow, and led me out onto the tarmac. He tossed my bag in the back, helped me up over the wing into the copilot's seat, and—I had begun to suspect this—climbed into the pilot's seat and revved the motor. I was glad the plane was new enough that someone did not have to get out and turn the propeller first. I had an idea who that would have been.

I tightened my seat belt and closed my eyes.

The flight to Columbia was surprisingly pleasant. At first I was disconcerted by how low we were flying and how closely we seemed to be following Highway 40 out of St. Louis. When it made a right turn, we made a right turn. However, it was such a reasonable approach to the problems of navigation that I soon relaxed and enjoyed the flight—no lectures from stewardesses on oxygen masks (we were 1200 feet up) or life jackets for crossing the Great Lakes ("That's the Missouri River," said the pilot/steward/ticket agent as the air currents gave us a jolt), no climbing through worrisome cloud banks (they were all far above us).

Make no mistake. I was delighted to get back on the ground and vowed never again to give money to any airline that employed leather-jacketed counter clerks. But it had been exhilarating, a sense of "really flying"—or maybe I should say really whizzing along Highway 40.

Most of those little airlines have grown up, and even *they* have twelve-seater planes and a steward aboard. And the airports are sprawling cities. You are likely to arrive at Gate D-16 at O'Hare with about forty-five minutes to reach Gate B-18. Only the hardiest—or perhaps the fool-hardiest—traveler will allow the travel agent to book a connecting flight through O'Hare.

I was doubly apprehensive when I planned a trip to Europe, where I would live for a year. I was going to fly from Kansas City to Chicago and somehow get all of my suitcases from the domestic terminal over to the international terminal for a flight to Frankfurt, an airport I had been told was even grander than O'Hare. To put this account into more painful perspective, I was hobbling about on crutches, a result of that fractured kneecap sustained in the line of duty at our university art museum.

A last-minute change of plans and an available seat on Iceland-air from Chicago to Luxembourg City was welcome. I had been to the Luxembourg Airport before. It was small enough for a man on crutches to manage the short walk from the gate through Customs to the car rental counter.

Breaking down through the clouds we saw the green Belgian and Luxembourgian countryside, then the tiny airport. Our wheels touched, and we taxied toward the terminal. Or so I thought. When the plane rolled to a stop, I looked out the window and was dismayed to discover that we were a good quarter of a mile from the terminal. To all my questions the stewardesses, who had been chatting away in pleasant, slightly accented English across the At-lantic, now reverted to their native dialect impenetrable to the out-sider. *If* they explained why we could barely see the terminal in the distance, I certainly never understood it. However, they were alert to my problem and radioed for a wheelchair to be brought out to the plane.

Needless to say, all the other passengers were well along on their trek before a man arrived at the foot of the stairs with a wheel-chair. He was short, stout, gray-haired, and dressed in blue cov-eralls. He motioned me to the chair; I sank in gratefully, crutches like a mast in front of me. The hot sun warmed us both as he pushed me from the steps of the boarding ramp across the tarmac on the long journey to the terminal building.

My attempts at light conversation brought only rapid French re-sponses. My occasional sorties in French produced a puzzled expression on his face and then a word or two in English. We agreed that it was hot. "*Très* chaud." That the walk was long—"loin." But most of the time I was saying, "Je ne comprends pas," and he was saying, "Répétez, s'il vous plaît."

He pushed me up to the end of the queue for Passport Control and then lit a well-earned cigarette. When we had cleared Passport Control, he wheeled me to the baggage reclaim counter where my fellow passengers were assembled to await their luggage. He smoked another cigarette. I explained as best I could how he could identify my bags—"un bleu et un brun." But *canvas*? He said, "D'accord," but I think that was just a Gallic pleasantry. We waited. It was now almost forty minutes since he had been detached to collect me at the plane. I had gathered from observing the mechanics and baggage handlers in their blue coveralls out on the runway and around the airport terminal building that my man's work was normally out there in the hot sun. When I begged his pardon for keeping him so long, he lit another cigarette and explained (I think) that he would only be hauling machines or lifting crates out in the heat. We smiled in complicity at each other and waited.

Of course, mine were the last suitcases to come sliding along the baggage carousel. But we had no difficulties at Customs. I suppose most smugglers would try to be *in*conspicuous. Here I was, crutches waving around in front, a baggage handler pushing my wheelchair and now towing a baggage cart behind him. Come to think of it, that would not be a bad cover.

Customs cleared, I now announced that I had to change some dollars into Belgian francs. He sighed deeply, turned our various vehicles around, and took us *back* through Passport Control, through a hallway and over to an elevator. Up we went, I changed my money, and we retraced our path through Passport Control again. I was by now somewhat embarrassed to be taking so much of his time. But I still needed to get to the car rental counter.

"The Car Rental Companies," he explained in the combination sign language and Franglais we had by this time worked out, "are outside the terminal, and I am not allowed to take the wheelchair outside." I had heard the guard at Customs tell him this, so I knew it was true. About two blocks away I could see the flashy signs for Hertz and Avis and Europcar. We considered the situation. He smoked another cigarette while I calculated distances. I suggested that if he would keep an eye on the baggage, I would wheel myself out there—or hobble on the crutches—across the road and up the little hill to Europcar.

"Non," he said, with finality, and stubbed out the last fragment of the cigarette. He had decided for us. "I will do it."

"I don't want to get you into trouble."

He shrugged, then spat on the floor. I could see he had no great love for authority.

And so we began the final leg (I use the term loosely) of our travels through the Luxembourg Airport. Out the door. Me in front, crutches rampant, then the baggage handler pushing me and pulling the baggage cart.

After a slow half block he had a better idea. And now I was certain that his normal work had to do with those trains of containers meeting incoming planes or loading the outgoing ones. He placed the cart with my suitcases in front, took my crutches from me and laid them out on the suitcases like a prow. Then aligning my wheelchair right behind the baggage, he instructed me to put my hands on the cart handle. He got behind my chair, and off we went like a little train with its engine in the rear. He was pushing me, and I was pushing the baggage cart. We were quite a spectacle, and heads were turning everywhere.

About fifty yards from the car rental offices we started up a small incline. We were going slower and slower, and my locomotive was growing noisier and noisier. It was really alarming. There was a kind of rattling in his chest just before our entourage came to a halt. "Un moment," he gasped.

I offered to get out and walk from there, but he gestured, no, he would make it. I said I hoped he was all right.

At this he snorted and said, "Regardez, monsieur." He unzipped the top of his coveralls and bared his chest down to the navel, pointing proudly at an angry scar—fairly recent, I should think—which began at his breast bone and meandered around his ribs and under his armpit. I was appalled. "Le coeur," he panted.

Good grief, I thought. I should get up and switch places with this man. Here was a recent open-heart-surgery patient about to keel over while pushing me for hours the length and breadth of the Luxembourg Airport—and the last two blocks illegally. However, he grunted, zipped up the evidence, took a deep, labored breath, and made it to the finish line fifty yards away.

Transferring all my suitcases into the rented car, he gathered the empty baggage cart and the vacant wheelchair for the much easier return run to the terminal, where he would have to negotiate as best he could with the authorities.

I pulled out my wallet, newly stocked with francs. What do you tip a man who has spent the last two hours risking his job and his life for you? I finally peeled off the equivalent of $20 in Belgian francs (and at two cents a franc that's a lot of peeling) and handed it to him. He looked happy.

We shook hands, said our adieus, and he set off downhill with his empty train. For days afterwards I searched anxiously the inner pages of the Luxembourg and Belgian newspapers for obituaries of airport workers in Luxembourg.

As a direct result of this nerve-wracking drama I decided to avoid those "little" airports and their short walks. Instead, I go outside and wait for the Red Bus. At least it won't be on *my* conscience if the driver cashes in his chips between here and Terminal C.

MY ITALIAN FIASCO
ARRIVEDERCI, TREZZO

I suppose every family has its own special places—those where marvelous memories began and those where disaster struck or was at least imminent. For some reason northern Italy, an area rich in art, history, food, home of friendly inhabitants, has always been a symbol of disaster for our family. Correct that: for me. My wife resolutely maintains she loved northern Italy.

With our three children we were driving east to Venice from Padua, and the trip went on and on. Darkness came. We drove on. Finally we pulled to the side of the road and switched on the overhead light to study our *Blue Guide to Italy*. There was no way that this trip could be taking three hours. We recalled the town we had just passed. And the one before that. We checked the map. Amid a few recriminations (and I think it is unnecessary to discuss who had been mapreader) we both realized we had been driving in a leisurely circle with a 50-mile diameter for the last hour and a half.

We reached the outskirts of Venice relatively quickly—if silently—after that roadside conference. I blush to admit what comes next, but it must be admitted. Although I had always known Venice as the city of canals, I thought one could drive *into* the city. So I kept circling the area where the ferries were loading passengers, seeking that elusive highway from Mestre to Venice. Our third time over the route, people lined up for the ferry began waving to us. The fourth time they cheered. That's when I gave up.

I pass over the pleasant three days we actually spent in Venice, our car hidden away in a car park near the ferry slip in Mestre. What our family remembers most vividly is the morning we picked up our pariah automobile from its kennel and began our rapid escape on the autostrada along the north of Italy, heading toward Milan. This time I think it is perfectly appropriate to specify that my wife was driving, while I glanced occasionally at the map,

which indicated a straight run from Mestre past Bergamo, Monza, and Milan.

About twenty minutes into her stint at the wheel, we both began to smell smoke. As we discussed pulling to the side of the road, we found that the brakes were not working. And when she tried to put the handbrake on, that's when we realized the handbrake *was* on, had been on since we had switched drivers twenty minutes ago. Fortunately, we saw a service area with gas station just ahead and managed, handbrake now off, to coast, smoking, to a stop well away from the gas pumps. We were immediately surrounded by a host of attendants and interested spectators pointing at the bottom of our car, gesticulating with great animation, and discussing rapidly with each other in Italian the underside of our car from which smoke—"fumo"—and the unpleasant smell of burnt rubber were emanating.

While all this was going on, I was frantically scouring my little Italian-English dictionary for the words to explain, "Mia sposa was driving—condotta." Fortunately the language barrier kept them from asking and me from having to explain what had caused our smelly and smoky intrusion into their service area. After some consultation it was clear to them all, and they managed to make it clear to us that the brake shoes were gone and that we would have to have new ones made. Because this was a Sunday afternoon, nothing could be done now, but in the nearby town to which we would be towed, there was a garage which could probably help us on Monday.

That is how we strayed from the normal tourist paths and found our way to Trezzo on the Adda River, a charming little town unaccustomed to foreign visitors. Actually the ride to Trezzo contributed another of our mottled memories of Italy.

The tow truck arrived. The driver, clearly a macho type with a cigarette dangling Jean-Paul Belmondo-style from his lip, surveyed the situation before hooking his chain under the rear bumper of our now totally disgraced car. He hoisted the rear end up in the air and then inspected my family. There I was—having now committed to memory the Italian version of "my wife was driving"—mia sposa herself, plus three bambinas ranging in age from three to thirteen. And he decided that *I* should ride in the truck with him while wife and bambinas rode backwards in the towed car along the shoulder of the autostrada.

"No," I announced, arriving belatedly at a proper view of a husband and father's protective role. "Pericolo." (My vocabulary was increasing rapidly.) "Pericolo," I repeated, pointing at the suspended car. "Danger."

"No pericolo," he said through the dangling cigarette.

But I was adamant and climbed into the driver's seat of my car. Much to his disgust (and probably shame) he had to allow a woman and three daughters into the cab of his tow truck. We set off.

As we eased onto the shoulder of the autostrada, I was terribly self-conscious. Fiats and Alfa Romeos were whizzing by at 130, 150 kilometers an hour, and there we were puddling along the side of the road at 30 or 40. More important, there I was, riding backwards and having to put up with the wide grins the drivers flashed as they zipped past. They waved and waggled their fingers at me. It was all friendly: I don't *think* there was an obscene gesture in the bunch. But it was still very embarrassing. I picked up a day-old *International Herald Tribune* from the seat beside me and mimed reading for the twenty-minute drive to Trezzo. Childish, I know, but it must have given a start to one or two of those Gran Prix drivers to see someone reading a newspaper while riding backwards on the autostrada.

We were towed to the garage and made some arrangements (I'm

still not sure what they were exactly, but we did get the car repaired in two days) with the owner, who had been dragged from his Sunday dinner to see these strange Americans and their burnt-out *frenos*. He even arranged to have us taken to the hotel.

It was a very attractive hotel—*albergo*—but nobody spoke English. Despite the fact that the hotel owner appeared to be related to the garage owner (it *was* a small town), the prices were very reasonable.

After washing up we went downstairs to see if we could get something to eat. The dining room would not open for another two hours, but the manager indicated that we could be served now. So there we were—five lost Americans sitting by ourselves at a round table in the midst of an empty dining room in a small hotel in Trezzo sul Adda.

There were no menus. Our waiter smiled continually but spoke no English. Our children were hungry, the three-year-old rather vocally. With a sporadic, hit-and-miss approach to the problem the friendly waiter and I agreed upon *uova*—eggs. It is needless to go into the undignified charades by which I emulated a chicken and its production methods. It is enough to say that he and I understood one another. He beamed at me. My children were quite impressed. Even my wife, the *condottore* of our earlier disaster, seemed to be getting over her chilliness at being singled out in the one Italian sentence I had attempted so far.

The type of food settled, the waiter now—pencil poised—asked, "Quanti?"

Well, I knew right away he wanted to know how many eggs, and I, made confident by our earlier rapport, snapped back immediately in my best Marcello Mastroianni accent: "Cento." (I wished I had thought to drape my sports jacket over my shoulders instead of actually wearing it.)

The waiter was clearly startled. He is probably, I thought, surprised at my new fluency. I had not even hesitated in pronouncing "chento" instead of "sento" as some foreigner might have done.

"Cento?" he repeated.

"Si," I replied. It was getting easier and easier.

"Cento uova, signor?" he asked slowly and, even I could tell, doubtfully.

"Si," I answered, "cento uova."

He was now regarding the five of us around the table and was rather obviously counting us.

My wife reached into my pocket for the little dictionary. "I think," she said, "that you have got something wrong." I was beginning to suspect so myself.

The three-year old was growing louder.

"Cento uova," the waiter said, writing slowly in his pad.

I was feeling a bit nervous by now, and I tried to make it all clear to him. I pointed to my wife and announced "uno"; this seemed to go over well enough so I showed off a bit. I pointed to my children in turn: "due, tre, quattro . . ." and then to myself. . . .

Just as I said proudly, "cento," and he said simultaneously "cinque," my wife found what she had been looking for in the dictionary.

"You have just," she said with an unsuppressed giggle, "ordered one hundred eggs."

To make a long story short (and this is one which I'd like to), the poor waiter, having had no previous experience with American guests, must have been considering whether this seemingly innocuous family of five could actually put away one hundred eggs. He had probably been calculating rapidly how the villagers could pool their resources and urge their hens into faster production.

I didn't mind so much the barely concealed titters of my wife and two older daughters. I *was* unnerved, however, at the number of times the kitchen door opened a crack, and a new face—a chef, a waiter, a scullery maid—peeped out at us, grinned broadly, and popped back into the kitchen.

The *cinque uova* came and were speedily dispatched. We did not linger over our coffee.

We remained two days in the hotel and were met everywhere with all-too-friendly smiles from the entire staff—from the desk clerk to the chambermaids. If we had had brake shoes, we would have fled in the dark of the first night.

When our car *was* fitted out with new brake shoes, we settled our bill at the hotel, loaded our suitcases, and prepared to depart. All the employees came out to see us off. Amid the repeated shouts of "buona fortuna" and "buon viaggio," I also heard a few giggles and a muted chorus of "cento uova, cento uova." We knew as we headed back toward the autostrada that we had become a legend in the little town of Trezzo sul Adda, and we pity any Americans who have since then wandered off the main routes to that pleasant small hotel. They could never have understood why everyone they met was grinning at them and muttering "cento uova, cento uova" each time they passed.

My daughters are all grown up now. But the one who was three at the time keeps urging me: "Tell the story about the hundred eggs, Daddy. Please." Of course I do, but it hurts when I observe across the room *mia sposa* still chuckling quietly to herself.

THE V SIGN AND OTHER
OLD-WORLD DRIVING HAZARDS

Not everyone will have to replace an automobile's smoking brake shoes in some tiny Italian hideaway, but I cannot imagine any American driving abroad who will not encounter an adventure or two—misreading an International Driving Sign or filling the gas tank for the first time in a foreign country. The foreign country, of course, does not know that it is a foreign country, and it is quite disconcerting to discover that *you* are the foreigner. Americans have never handled this kind of foolishness well.

Some years ago, before self-service gasoline stations became common in the United States, I ran into my first one in The Hague. Unfortunately, not only was it the first time I had ever served myself, but it was the first gasoline needed by my brand-new Volkswagen Rabbit. I checked my Owner's Manual to find out the gas tank capacity. (Scholars *do* like to work from a text.) Ten and six-tenths gallons. No problem. Without much difficulty I located the gas cap on my car. Then I looked at the Dutch gas pump. The fuel was not measured in gallons but in liters, and I did not have the foggiest idea how many liters there were in a gallon—or was it how many gallons in a liter?

Not only that, but the liters were being charged, of course, in guilders. The Dutch attendant sitting inside the office at the cash register must have wondered why it was taking fifteen minutes to fill up a Volkswagen, but he could not know that I was translating the mounting guilders into dollars and then pausing to translate dollars into gallons before I worked out my estimate about how much gasoline might be inside the tank now. By the time I got the gas cap back on and handed over the appropriate number of guilders, I was exhausted and would have traded my car even up for a Eurailpass.

This desire to rid oneself of an automobile may come upon a driver almost anywhere. Even more frustrating than The Hague was my experience late one December afternoon in the ancient Galilean city of Nazareth.

Living in London on sabbatical, I had been idly glancing through the travel section of the *Times* one Sunday morning when I saw an advertisement for a winter Getaway Tour to Israel. None of those "Weekend in Denver!" or "Three Days, Two Nights in Historic Natchez" with which travel agents generally lure Kansans off the prairies. No, this was Religion, Culture, History—Masada, Jericho, the Dead Sea—and all for £1000. Yes, the travel agent said, my wife and I could fly from Luton Airport north of London to Ben Gurion Airport outside Tel Aviv, enjoy seven nights of lodgings and some meals at kibbutzim anywhere in the country, plus have an automobile with unlimited mileage. And, yes, all for £1000.

I must admit I had some worries about bombs, invasions, and the legendary maniacs cruising the Israeli highways. But my unruffled travel agent urged a fatalistic approach to the first two anxieties and took a pragmatic approach to the third.

"The Israelis," he said, "do not think anything of passing four or five cars at a time." I did not think much of it either.

"Ever since the Six Day War," he went on, "they figure that anyone who could drive tanks through the Sinai can handle a passenger car on a highway." I looked dubious. "Just take the extra insurance," he said. "The Israeli hospitals are among the best in the world."

So I handed over my Barclaycard as ransom, and the December trip began to take shape. I had a few bad moments just prior to take-off. As I was washing my hands in the men's room near the boarding area, a fellow passenger pointed to what looked like an empty Coca Cola can above the sink. "Don't move," he ordered. I stopped in mid-rinse. Feeling gingerly around the can, he pronounced it "an empty coke can." What am I doing, I thought, going to a country where coke cans might be something else? I was about to telephone my travel agent to see if the Majorca tour was still open, but they were calling my flight.

Driving around the small country proved much less frightening than the prospect of it. We had been warned that the Arabs would throw rocks at our car in the Occupied Territory, and the Orthodox Jews would throw rocks if we drove on the Sabbath, so we warily picked our way between Scylla and Charybdis (they are on the road to Beersheba). Oh, we did get splattered by an eggplant as we ignored some roadside vendors, but I suspect that was more a commercial response than a political or religious one.

Where we ran into trouble was the sharp right turn we took shortly after leaving the Church of the Annunciation in Nazareth. My wife was driving, and I was reading the map.

"Make an almost-hairpin right turn," I told her, "and we can look at some of the old city before we leave town."

Dutifully, she made the prescribed turn and steered along a narrow one-way, one-lane street lined with stone houses. In the twilight, the street seemed to be growing even narrower. It also appeared to have deteriorated from "street" to a pair of thin concrete strips with a two-foot ditch between them. We were driving over a pit! One false move would plunge us in. Behind us, another car was moving slowly, and ahead the "roadway" ended where a man stood washing his car.

Unable to go forward, we stopped. So did the automobile which had followed us down the narrowing track. Three young Arabs emerged from it, and one of them opened the hood and was apparently scrutinizing the inner workings of the engine while the other two looked on. I would have been worried in New York City or Chicago; trapped at a pit stop in Nazareth, I felt the adrenalin surging.

Two of the young men got back into the car and, under the guidance of the one who stayed outside, managed to back the car out and turn it around. I was relieved. The remaining young man watched our futile efforts to get our own car backed up without dropping it into the pit. I had stepped out to analyze our problem from behind the car. It was not an encouraging sight. As my wife attempted to carry out my shouted instructions, we covered a few hectic yards in reverse.

It could not have been easy for her. I tried to sound authoritative and reassuring:

"Left. NO! Right. . . . No. Stop. STOP!"

She turned the ignition off and gave me what at best can be called a withering stare. *If* we got out of Nazareth, it was doubtful that our marriage would last the long drive back to Jerusalem.

The young Arab who had been observing it all, pointed at the car, now perched precariously, with a rear wheel on the ledge. "You want I drive?" he inquired, making steering-wheel motions with his hands. He was actually offering to back the car out for us. I went to the front and presented this proposal to the frazzled driver. She jumped out with alacrity, and this young man, this stranger we had not seen ten minutes earlier, whom, I am sorry to say, we had been eyeing nervously, now sat behind the wheel, took one quick estimate out the rear window, whipped the car into reverse, and, with nary a false move, backed it out to where the roadway began, turned it around, aimed it in the proper direction, and got out. I admit to one more unworthy fear as he headed it away from us: I would never see my rented car again. (I'm not sure I would have cared all that much.) But, no. He handed the keys back and absolutely refused the money I was guiltily trying to offer him. He smiled gently and said, "No, no."

Amid a sprinkling of "Salams" we headed out of Nazareth, wiser in the ways of the Middle East than we had been before.

The ways of Europe and Great Britain also took a bit of getting used to. Through an Audi dealer in Kansas City, I had arranged to take delivery of a new car in Frankfurt. When I first picked the car up, I did not really have an opportunity to see how fast it would go. The German dealer was puzzled by my question about a break-in period.

"Should I keep it under a certain speed?" I wanted to know.

"Ach, ja," he said after a moment's thought. "For the first 500 kilometers you should not make it to go faster than 120 kilometers an hour."

I nodded my head in apparent comprehension, but it was not until I had reached the glistening new silver-grey Audi and was turning the key in the ignition that I worked out the kilometers per hour to miles per hour. The dealer had just told me not to go over 75 miles an hour. Had he forgotten that I came from America where, in its wisdom, the federal government would not allow me and my countrymen to exceed 55 miles per hour? I had not driven 75 miles per hour in seven or eight years.

Well, I eased that brand-new power plant out onto the autobahn heading north toward Belgium, and I moved her up to a smooth, effortless 110 kilometers per hour. Anyone who has ever driven on an autobahn knows what happened next. Mercedes, BMWs, and even little Volkswagens were passing me—rapidly. I nudged her up to 120. Some of the Volkswagens tailed off, but the BMWs and the Mercedes still came roaring up to my bumper, flashed their bright lights at me insistently until I was shamed into the slow lane, and then went zooming past, a contemptuous sneer on the driver's face. Hobbled by my breaking-in instructions, I had to decline all challenges to dogfights on the autobahn. I dawdled along at 120 kph until I reached Dunkerque and made my escape.

In Great Britain, of course, the speed limits are in miles, and the authorities are strict about enforcing them: 70 mph on the motorways and lower on the secondary roads. I reached 75 miles an hour only for a short stretch between Manchester and Sheffield, and that was in the dusk with the light behind me.

Surely some time before the Audi was put out to pasture at 55 miles per hour back in the U.S.A. I had to give it its head. The moment came on a long straightaway 50 kilometers north of Prague. Properly cowed by the barbed wire and machine-gun-toting East German border police, I had obeyed the speed limits along the poorly kept highways of the German Democratic Republic. The roads might not be well maintained, but I was positive the firearms were. When we left Dresden, however, and headed south toward Prague, I began to feel my spirits rise. The crossing from one Eastern European country to another was simple and unintimidating.

There seemed to be almost no traffic on the Czech highways, and I recalled a sentence I thought I had read in the guidebook we had collected with our visas back in London: "There are no speed limits on the highways in Czechoslovakia." It brought me back to the "Reasonable and Proper" limits Missouri used to apply to its roads in the fifties. Drivers with suicidal tendencies happily urged the speedometer over 100 whenever they felt such numbers to be "reasonable and proper." I might now be on the E15 behind the Iron Curtain, but in some kind of time warp it was 1954, and I was back on old Highway 40 flying toward Kingdom City.

In the rear seat my wife was stretched out sleeping peacefully. Up front my teenage daughter sat beside me.

"Would you like to see how fast this car will go?" I asked.

"Why not?" she said. "Is it legal?"

"No problem. There's no speed limit in Czechoslovakia."

And with that, I floored it. Oh, that Audi had been waiting a long time for this. The sneers and exhaust fumes of a hundred BMWs were forgotten. The snickers of haughty Mercedes and Porsches were erased. Like an eager test car on the desert proving grounds, the Audi headed toward the sound barrier while peasants working in the fields turned to stare at the silver bullet flying toward Prague. We had about a mile of straightaway, and the readings were pretty impressive—130, 135, 140, 145, 150, 155, 160 kilometers per hour—before the road began a gentle curve, and I reined the exultant Audi in. My daughter's smile was frozen on her face, both hands were clamped tightly to the grab bar, and her feet were braced against the dashboard. My wife slept on.

That evening in Prague we shared a table in a small, out-of-the-way restaurant with a Swiss businessman, fluent in many languages and knowledgeable in the ways of the Czechs. In the course of our conversation I expressed surprise at the lack of speed limits in Czechoslovakia.

"But," he interrupted, "there *is* a limit—100 kilometers per hour, 62 miles per hour."

I told him about airing it out on the E15. He whistled softly. I explained about the brochure which had convinced me that speed limits were unheard of on Czech highways. He was shaking his head in disbelief and began to recount horror stories of speeders who were still languishing in the dungeons of Brno or Bratislava. I sipped thoughtfully at my pilsener, recalling the open-mouthed wonder of the peasants by the roadside. Perhaps it had not been my dazzling speed and derring-do they had been marveling at.

Throughout the rest of the meal I was somewhat less animated than usual, but afterwards I asked our Swiss companion if he had a ride back to his hotel. No, he had been intending to call for a taxicab to take him to Wenceslas Square in the heart of Prague. Of course, I insisted that he let me drive him. There was a brief pause while he reflected on my racing tendencies. But he accepted my invitation and we wound down through the historic old city and reached the fashionable district where his first-class hotel was located. Ours was a mile or two away, along some trolley tracks and past a lot of torn-up streets.

On Wenceslas Square I stopped to let him out, and we said our goodbyes as he leaned in the window on the passenger side. When he stepped away into the night, I became aware of a car which had pulled up next to mine. A military man, a pistol strapped to his thigh, was approaching my window. He saluted me. This gesture was not reassuring: in all the spy movies I had ever seen, a salute always preceded the arrest—to say nothing of the execution. He addressed us in what I assumed was Czech. I shook my head and explained in English that I did not understand him. He shifted into a halting English.

"Your papers, please." My wife began to rummage through her handbag for our passports, visas, and automobile documents.

I gave him my friendliest, open, middle America smile, uncomfortably aware that I had stopped directly on a zebra-striped pedestrian crossing. I was also regretting my earlier folly in cracking the 160-kilometer barrier on the way into town.

"What are you doing here?" he wanted to know. With a sinking feeling I realized that my wife's continued forays into the deeper reaches of her purse indicated that the required documents were not there. I had to buy some time.

"What do you mean 'here'?" I asked him. "Here in Prague or here in Wenceslas Square?" God help me, I was having a metaphysical discussion with a soldier who had a pistol strapped to his trouser leg. The counter-offensive, however, seemed to puzzle him, and I guessed that his English was confined to relatively straightforward topics. "Or here in this car?" I added with wild abandon.

My wife had turned her handbag inside out and was now reconnoitering the glove compartment.

He and I were both watching her with diminishing hope. "Where in Prague do you stay?" the soldier wanted to know. He was obviously discouraged about the earlier line of inquiry.

Fortunately, I had a card from the Hotel Opera and handed it to him. He examined it quickly, observed my wife's new offensive upon her handbag, shook his head in defeat, and saluted me once more.

"That is all," he said. "Good night."

We never did know whether our innocence was evident on our honest Kansas faces or whether there is a fatal weakness in the Czech character. Perhaps, we thought later, our Swiss business-man friend had been lurking in the darkness and had given some sign to the soldier. Perhaps he had not been a Swiss businessman at all.

Early the next morning we packed quickly and left Prague, creeping toward the Austrian border at a steady 98–99 kilometers per hour. After a few carefree days of Viennese tortes, kaffee, und musik it was time to turn north along the German autobahns and head for the Channel ports and England. I set the Cruise Control at 130 and rolled into Boulogne ahead of most of the other cars on the highway. But it wasn't the same: my thirst for the fast lane had been slaked in Czechoslovakia. Too many fantasies about the Czech prison system, I suppose.

In Great Britain, however, there were adventures which had nothing to do with speed. Obviously, when you have grown up, as Americans have, knowing that God ordained left-hand drives for automobiles, you have a few difficult adjustments to make in a country where such verities are not recognized.

For instance, the first time I saw what I thought was the driver of a cruising Morris Minor reading the *Guardian*, I almost went off the road. It was, of course, the passenger who was reading while the driver paid attention to his job. British roundabouts—traffic circles—have an etiquette all their own which the unwary American may never quite master. You do not sidle into them slowly: you *wait*. And wait. Any automobile already on the roundabout has the right-of-way and will not merge with just any pushy outsider. On the other hand, U- turns are legal on almost any road, no matter how heavily traveled. Accustomed to the less imaginative regulations of my own country, I was excited by this new freedom and often went out of my way to make U-turns on most of the major thoroughfares of London—Pall Mall, Finchley Road, the Brompton Road, and the Edgware Road. I used to collect them.

By the time I went on my most recent sabbatical I had made most of the U-turns and had, I thought, learned all of the international road signs and the peculiarly British ones like "Humps for ½ Mile" and "Loose Chippings." However, driving through Cheltenham in late afternoon traffic one Friday, I encountered a new one.

I was halted in a long line. Behind me was a Volvo lorry straining at its brakes. All the cars ahead began to move forward except the Ford Cortina directly in front of me. The Volvo lorry produced a few ear-splitting blasts on its air horn, and the driver of the Ford in front turned around and shook a fist at me, apparently assuming that I was the one who had emitted that bellowing bray of the wild bull elephant. I shrugged and smiled. He moved up ten feet. We all did. In a few minutes, the queue moved forward once again. Except the Ford. I figured he was having engine problems so I simply pulled out and zipped around him into the space ahead.

You would not think that such an innocent action could rouse such fury. The little Ford was apoplectic. It pulled up almost onto my bumper, its high-pitched horn beeping irately at me. In surprise, I turned around to see what the problem might be and discovered the choleric driver rapping his horn, shaking his fist, and then flashing me the old Winston Churchill V Sign. Although I was uncertain how this split-fingered gesture was relevant for our street encounter and despite a few misgivings—I checked to make sure that there was only one chap in the Ford and not four teenage louts—I returned him the V for Victory.

This reminder of our wartime alliance—Edward R. Murrow, Lend-Lease, and all that—seemed to drive him quite insane. He leaned on his horn and was obviously shouting unpleasant things at me. I finally made it through the long bottleneck, reached the outskirts of historic Cheltenham, and headed for London on the A40. The Ford Cortina was still with me! The inflamed driver was hammering away at his horn and occasionally roaring right up to my rear bumper to get his point across—whatever that might be. I thought I would lose him when I left Cheltenham and its environs, but he continued to attack for three miles out on the London Road. I was about to give him the Peace sign to calm him down. Fortunately, I remembered in time: it was the same V sign which had gotten me into all this trouble in the first place.

With a final blast on his overworked horn and one last close encounter with my tailpipe, the angry driver peeled off on the road to Dowdeswell.

Puzzled by the strange reaction of this madman to my simple returned gesture, I casually inquired of a few English friends over dinner if they could understand why the man had been so exercised. They were amused but slightly embarrassed by my question. Later, one of them took me aside privately.

"Look," he said, "it's a bit dicey."

"What is?"

"Well, you see, it wasn't Winston Churchill, and it wasn't the Peace Sign." I had gathered as much. "In both of those," he continued, "the palm faces outward. Did you happen to notice when he first leaned on his hooter and signaled to you?"

No, I hadn't. I had looked around, and there he was giving me the V for Victory. Returning it, I had simply held up my hand as I was driving ahead of him.

"It would have been the back of your hand then?"

"Yes, I suppose so."

Well, as you will have guessed, there was something decidedly rude, as the English would say, about a V Sign offered with the back of one's hand. Evidently, my antagonist and I had been communicating the same message Americans transmit with a single digit. I was horrified. In my own country I would certainly not cruise the mean streets bandying obscene gestures with possibly psychopathic drivers.

Now I recalled a story former Kansas football coach Pepper Rodgers used to tell on himself. One very long afternoon at Memorial Stadium, arch-rival Missouri was piling it on, and Pepper claims to have caught the eye of Dan Devine, the Missouri coach. "I gave him the Peace Sign," Pepper said, "but he only returned half of it."

Had I remembered the Dan and Pepper exchange sooner, I might have avoided playing tag on the A40 out of Cheltenham. As it was, I inserted a new Road Hazard sign to memorize in the chart of International Driving Symbols pasted to the wall of my London flat.

Peace.

PERIL ON THE SEA

Although I have had my exciting moments driving in England and on the Continent, transporting my automobile from Europe to the plains of Kansas has provided its own special tensions.

The Volkswagen of my first sabbatical—the one that foolishly kept seeking an overland route into Venice, the one that was towed backwards on the autostrada—that one made it across the ocean and as far as Illinois, where it was asked to pull a used ping-pong table (in a U Haul trailer, of course) back to Kansas. The indignity was too much for its little engine that couldn't. It turned out to be a $600 ping-pong table.

The Volkswagen Rabbit of my second sabbatical fared even worse. Fond memories of the first VW led to purchase of the second. When I picked it up in Luxembourg, I was dazzled by its shiny red exterior and the obviously more powerful engine. This one could probably pull a ping-pong table and a few paddles besides. I drove it north through France, ferried it across the Channel, and spent a cheery few months on the wrong side of the road in London. It did everything I asked without a whimper.

When it came time to cross to the Continent once again, it happily rejoined the cars on the right side of the road, zipped down the Atlantic coast of France, and curled along the hairpin curves of Spanish highways like a veteran Seat from Madrid or Segovia. Nary a scratch did it acquire in the downtown traffic of Granada or Cordoba.

Lisbon was to be the real test. I did not know that until I reached Lisbon, but a few minutes driving in the city was enough to convince me. When I come back in my next life, I want it to be as a man completely without fear, without any niggling doubts: I want to come back as a Lisbon taxi driver. I want to be able to take my car from 0 to 60 on a downtown street in 8 seconds. Or even 9.

Opening a little window among the fingers that were covering my eyes, I saw our first driver aim at—and then miss by a few inches—two young women crossing the street. My heart sank when I saw a slower-moving nun in the pedestrian crossing a scant hundred feet ahead. However, he slowed a few feet from her, stopped, stuck his head out the window, and smiled a friendly "Buon día" to her. The Church may be losing its sway in some countries, but obviously not in Portugal. Anyway, a few such trips caused paralysis to set in every time I had to take my own little red Rabbit. Not to worry. They never laid a glove on it.

As a matter of fact, that car was still unscratched the day it was time to take it down to the docks in London for its sea voyage to the New World. We said our goodbyes and promised to meet in Chicago in a few weeks.

Two weeks after I reached Kansas I began expecting word of our freighter's arrival or at least of its successful passage through the St. Lawrence Seaway. Three weeks passed. I decided to call the phone number in Chicago.

To my query of whether or not the Angina Doria had arrived in port, a pleasant woman replied, after a moment of checking that, yes, it had. To my question of whether or not my little red Rabbit was ready for pickup she was less forthcoming. She suggested I call back in a couple of days.

Unable to imagine what the problem might be, I waited. When I called back, she was still pleasant but evasive. I finally elicited from her the information that my automobile had been "damaged."

"Damaged? How can that be? What happened?"

"I'm sorry," she said, "but I don't have any information on it other than that it has been damaged. . . ."

"But how badly? I mean, can I drive it?"

"I'm sorry, sir, but you'll have to wait until the insurance adjuster has finished his inspection. Can you call back tomorrow?"

After a bad night thinking of that poor lone VW, sitting wounded on the pier in Chicago, I telephoned the following day. When I pressed my point about how badly the car had been damaged—a broken windshield, perhaps?—she admitted reluctantly that it had been "totaled." I was stunned.

"Totaled?" I repeated after her. "Totaled? How can it be totaled crossing the Atlantic? How can it be totaled in the St. Lawrence Seaway? What are you saying to me?"

This barrage of anguished questions was obviously unfair to the poor young woman, who was after all only the messenger. She waited until I ran down. "A load of steel beams got loose," she said softly, "and damaged a number of cars in the hold."

"Totaled," I murmured.

"Well," she added, trying to be helpful, "it wasn't as badly smashed as some of the others. The Jaguar next to it was squashed to sixteen inches high."

At the moment of my agony I found little comfort in this comparative damage report. Totaled is totaled. She suggested now that I get in touch with the insurance adjuster who had been inspecting the situation in the last day or two. It took me a few days just to run him down: apparently he plies the Seaway—a kind of freighter chaser—handling the big accidents like bridge-brushings and barge-sinkings along with the minor claims which I soon realized was my league.

Had he seen my red Volkswagen? He had. Unscathed in all its European wanderings, it had not been able to make it across the ocean. I suppose I was beginning to face that fact now because I wanted to know more about the accident in general. He told me. I recalled the secretary's attempt at solace—the Jaguar that had been reduced to sixteen inches high. "Is that true?" I asked him.

"No," he said, "it isn't. It wasn't a Jaguar. It was a Mercedes. And it wasn't sixteen inches. It was eighteen." I guessed he'd be a whiz on insurance claims, but I thought the friendly secretary had grasped the main point well enough.

I had purchased the Volkswagen in March. It had died in July. It took me more than seven months to get my insurance claim paid off—longer than the short happy life it had enjoyed. Somehow we lacked a vital piece of the original contract issued by the German insurance firm in quadruplicate back in March. I was invited to read the fine print in that part of the contract I did have. Unfortunately the fine print was in German Gothic.

I spent a goodly amount of time sending affidavits back and forth between Kansas and Marburg and Wolfsburg and München. It was ultimately a sad day when the check for the full amount of the totaled vehicle finally reached me. It wasn't just that in the intervening period the Deutschmark had risen 25 percent against the dollar, so that the lost VW was worth more than the insurance amount. It was my unkept promise to meet it in Chicago.

For my next sabbatical, I vowed I would purchase a rail pass for travel in Europe. I didn't think my spirit could handle another shipwreck.

AN ALIEN IN LONDON

SABBATICAL PROJECTS
LEARNING THE LANGUAGE
AND READING THE NATIVES

If they are lucky, academics are awarded a seventh year off from their teaching duties to engage in research or to travel. At my university only 4 percent of the faculty may be on sabbatical leave at the same time so professors compete to see who can most persuasively describe the wonders they will perform if they are granted a year's leave at half pay or, for the grasshoppers without savings accounts, a half year at full pay. They need to examine dusty manuscripts in forgotten Romanian archives, engage in equation-laden conversation with fellow physicists at international Quark Seminars, or study the social structures discernible among groups of headhunters hidden high in the Andes. I have never cared to study the headhunters, nor have I wished them to study me; my Romanian is rusty; my quark consciousness unraised. For my sabbatical projects I always paint the glorious results of research to be conducted in the more civilized confines of the British Museum, the Public Record Office, or the Palaeography Room at the University of London Library.

And so about every seven years (once or twice the Sabbaticals Committee opted for quarks instead), I have crossed the Atlantic to live with my family—or occasionally without—in England. They have been grand years marked by adventure and misadventure, broadening experiences which every middle American ought to have. They just don't do things the same way in England as in America. On more than a few occasions I found myself muttering, "Toto, I don't think we're in Kansas any more." The line drew a blank from all my English acquaintances.

As every schoolboy knows, the language is not the same. A few years ago during one of the periodic IRA bomb scares I drove my automobile up to the British Museum and wanted to park it in the courtyard. One of the guards allowed himself to be persuaded but first wanted me to open my bonnet. I offered him quite a few choices before he tapped the hood of my car. I unlocked it for him.

"Now, sir," he said after a brief inspection, "may I have a look in the boot?"

Although I made only two or three false moves before I worked it out that he meant the trunk, I overheard him mutter to his fellow guard: "This bloke doesn't know his boot from his bonnet." It seemed a fair assessment. Over the years there have been plenty of other discoveries. Putting the garbage out for the "dustmen" was a bit disconcerting, and so was being complimented by a friendly librarian on my "jumper." Back home, my daughters wear jumpers. She meant, of course, my sweater, a name that struck the librarian as being equally odd.

But it's more than the words themselves which make the visitor aware of his strangeness. It's the pronunciation, or perhaps more accurately, the music of the speech. Scotland and the north of England are almost impossible, but even in London translations are sometimes required. I still shudder when I recall my first sabbatical and the problems I had making myself understood. Each day at lunch time I used to walk out the front door of the British Museum, down the steps, and across Great Russell Street to the Museum Tavern, where I would order a pork pie or a Cornish pasty and a small glass of beer. I was aware, as only an alien can be, that the locals were not ordering a small beer: they were asking for "'alf a pint of bitter" (when they weren't ordering a pint—much more likely). "'Ahhhf a pint," is what they were saying. Day after day I ordered my small glass of beer, but secretly—at home in the morning while I shaved or late at night just before I turned out the lights—I was practicing.

"'Ahhhf a pint of bitter," I would say to my approving English mirror. "Right you are, guv'nor," it would respond obligingly. After three weeks of such mirrored rapport I thought I was ready to take on the publican at the Museum Tavern. We were all bellying up to the bar (there *must* be an English equivalent, but I never learned it), pressing for our sandwiches, pies, and brew. The queuing

which marks other aspects of British life is nonexistent in a pub at lunchtime. Suddenly, I was in front of the taps.

"What'll it be, guv'nor?" the barman asked.

I was ready. I had been ready for the last five days. In my most practiced manner, I responded, "'Ahhhf a pint of bitter, please."

He looked up sharply. But I was not worried because, like Eliza Doolittle at Ascot, I was sure I had got it right.

Then he said, "'Ahhhf a pint of *wot*, guv'nor?"

He destroyed me, of course.

"I'll have a small glass of beer, please," I answered. So ended my doomed attempt to pass for a native.

Although I never repeated my "'ahhhf a pint" fiasco, I did continue to study local culture in the public houses of London. Recently, in a Hampstead pub quaintly named the Old Boar and Bush I was sitting quietly when a slightly balding, not-quite-young man caught my eye and began to talk to me. For a scholar who had been studying the accents the way I had, spotting him for an Irishman was a cinch. His name, he said, was Brian. What was mine? I told him, and we were good friends. (The instant camaraderie confirmed his nationality: even in pubs the English are a bit reserved.) Brian was friendly, loquacious, and insisted upon buying me a pint. While we drank—Guinness, of course—he talked about Ireland and the absolute necessity that I see it. I told him I thought I would. Such an idle conversational gambit probably passes unnoticed hundreds of times in a night of tippling in Hampstead or in Kansas City, but it did not pass in The Old Boar and Bush that night.

"When will you be going?" Brian wanted to know. I waved my hand vaguely and said I did not know. He pressed me. "Maybe," I allowed, "in October or November," two safe months away.

"You'll stay with my mother," he announced.

"What are you talking about?"

"When you go to dear old Ireland. You'll stay at my mother's house. She lives just outside of Galway."

I dredged around in my mind for his name. "I can't do that," I said at last. "I don't know your mother."

"No matter," he replied. "You know me, and she'll be overjoyed to have you."

"Byron. . . ." I said.

"Brian."

"Brian. I have known you for fourteen minutes. Your mother is *not* going to be overjoyed to have me."

"Sure, and any friend of mine is welcome in Galway."

To his credit, Brian had no doubts about it. Before I sloshed out bleary from a mere three pints of Guinness, he had extracted a promise to stay with his sainted mother in Galway. Tomorrow night over a few more pints I would furnish the details of my Emerald Isle itinerary, and he would write straightaway to his mother who would begin to air the featherbeds.

These rapid developments saddened me because in only a few nights I had become very fond of The Old Boar and Bush. Fires blazed in its fireplaces, lager and bitter flowed freely from its taps, animated talk swirled in every corner. But the truth was that I had no plans to visit Ireland, and I certainly did not intend to descend upon Brian's mother. But I could not tell him that now. So I had to strike The Old Boar and Bush off my calling list, and I sighed each evening as I drove thirstily past on my way home from the dry and dusty British Museum.

While I might bypass the troublesome pubs, I could not ignore the banks of Britain, rather different institutions from those at home. All my half-salary checks from the State of Kansas had to be "negotiated" before Barclays Bank Limited would credit my account with pounds sterling. Reassuringly, behind all the paper transactions stood The Bank of England, known affectionately as "The Old Lady of Threadneedle Street." I tried to imagine an American bank being known affectionately. I gave up.

Banking itself is rather different in Britain. In the States I have never had much luck keeping my checkbook balanced; I have no chance at all with a chequebook. And years ago, when I opened my first chequing account—before decimalization—one did not simply add pounds in one column and pence in another (near enough to dollars and cents to keep an innumerate American reasonably close to a proper balance). No, the pounds were in one column, the shillings in another, and the pence in a third. When you reached so many pence (twelve was the nice round number they had come up with), you converted them to a shilling and added it to the shillings column; when you reached twenty shillings, you added a pound to the pounds column. Merely subtracting one cheque for eight pounds, three shillings, and eightpence (£8 3s. 8p.—or 8d., as they used to write it) from a balance of £127 2s. 5d. could bring on hyperventilation.

Happily, the British banks have always been more generous with credit than my Full Service Kansas bank, which *will* cover for my occasional mishaps but debits me $15 for each one and sniffs a bit at my grasshopper approach to financial affairs. But Midland and National Westminster and Barclays all treat overdrafts as a common and rather jolly occurrence. In a way, they have institutionalized check kiting. One holiday season when I had been a tad overspirited and overdrawn, I telephoned my Barclays branch office and explained that I would like to write more cheques than I had pounds and pence in my account. At home such an announcement would produce at least one "Tut-tut" or a disapproving "Hmmm" before a stiff vice president took pity on an improvident professor. Here, the response was friendly and non-judgmental:

"How much of an overdraft did you have in mind, sir?"

I had been planning to ask for £90 (it sounded like a lot less than £100), but the bank officer was so warm and encouraging that I heard myself answering "£150."

"Yes, sir," he said. "That will be fine." I thought so too.

The Barclay people have a Barclaycard, and they handle their credit limits with the same unstinting generosity. I applied for one and received a card with a credit limit of £300. With the pound then valued around $1.50 this worked out to about $450 and would not do at all. Not for a man whose chequebook balancing raised more questions than it answered. I made them a counter offer: How about £800? Done. By return post I had a new credit limit of £800. Unfortunately, the holiday season again proved my undoing, and in early January I received a letter from Barclaycard headquarters in the Midlands of England. I had exceeded my credit limit—I was now up to £802 47p. Consequently—I cringed, knowing full well what an American credit card company would be telling me at a juncture like this—consequently, it went on, "we are temporarily raising your credit limit to £850 and hope that this will prove satisfactory." My goodness, I thought, and here's a nation which has given us Chaucer and Milton and Shakespeare as well!

Another civilized feature of the banking system allows customers to cash cheques up to £100 anywhere in the country if they can show a bank card. And, rather than requiring you to open a new account at a new branch whenever you move, Barclays allows you to leave your account in one branch and cash your cheques regularly at another. What you do is set up an "Arrangement" with another branch for whatever amount per week you might like to cash. You can even manage this over the telephone.

"A hundred and twenty-five pounds a week?" I asked tentatively.

"Yes, sir," replied the clerk on the telephone.

It was slightly disconcerting the first time I tried this system out in the Golders Green branch where I intended cashing my cheques. I had forgotten the term—I thought it was "Agreement"—and when the pert young woman at the till looked at my cheque drawn on the British Museum Branch and asked suggestively, "Do you have an Arrangement?" I got all flustered. Finally, I stammered out an affirmative. After a suspiciously long time she came back waving the approved cheque.

"How do you want it?" she asked.

Shades of Leacock! but, alas, true: "In cash," I said.

"I know that," she answered pleasantly (the colonials do occasionally have a bit of a problem). "I meant what kind of banknotes?"

Having somehow survived that first encounter, I afterwards experienced a little *frisson* of pleasure whenever I slid a cheque across the counter and whispered breathily, "I have an arrangement."

I did have one cross-cultural misunderstanding with Barclays back in 1977 when I was coming home after living in a flat on Fellows Road in Swiss Cottage. Laboriously, I wrote out my instructions in a letter. "Please," I concluded, "send all future statements to me at the address on the other side." And, turning the sheet over, I carefully printed my address in Lawrence, Kansas, U.S.A.

Two months later at the tail-end of a sweltering Kansas summer I had completely forgotten my instructions to Barclays. One day there arrived an official envelope from Barclays Bank Limited. It had been addressed to me at 128 Fellows Road, Swiss Cottage, London, NW3, and had meandered across the Atlantic in the desultory way surface mail travels when it is forwarded at cheap rates.

"Dear Mr. Gold," it began. "Barclays would be happy to send statements to you at your new address, but you did not indicate what your address on the other side of the street would be." It was signed with one of those inscrutable English scribbles which defy surmises about sex or surname. For a long time I pondered whether or not I was dealing with a peculiarly English sense of humor or whether I had been especially opaque in my change-of-address letter in referring to "the other side." I finally decided to treat the Barclays missive as if it had been written by a roguish bank clerk although I had never in my life met or even heard tell of one.

I solved, rather neatly it seemed to me, the problem of determining who or what my correspondent was. I Xeroxed the signature twice, pasted one copy on my envelope, and wrote "Barclays Bank Limited" and the address beneath it. For my salutation, I wrote "Dear" and pasted in the Xeroxed name. Then I assured my unknown correspondent how much I appreciated his or her dry sense of humor, but, of course, I knew that he—or she—could not have failed to look "on the other side" of the *sheet*. Sheet, not street.

This brought a prompt air mail reply, signed in the same illegible scrawl, thanking me for my "jolly" letter, apologizing for the confusion, and inviting me on my next visit to London to join my still unnamed and ungendered friend for a pint at the pub "on the other side."

Fancy my Full Service Kansas Banker suggesting that!

ALIEN REGISTRATION AND
OTHER FORMALITIES

W henever I am on sabbatical in London, I do my best to shed my Kansas accent, dress like an Englishman, and generally fit in. Unfortunately, it's not easy to pass for a native when you have to carry an Alien Registration booklet. This is not a problem for the short-term tourist, but a stay longer than three months sends the overseas visitor with his passport down to Lamb's Conduit Street and the Alien Registration Office. There we all sit on benches, sliding along as police registrars listen to our claims and plans and keep calling out, "Next."

The last time I registered, I was shocked to find I had to pay £25 for what used to be free. A young official filled in my answers in the little booklet and stapled to it my dour-looking color photograph (Four Poses for 60 Pence! Bring a Friend!). I was not planning to enjoy the National Health Service or anything expensive like that so I asked her what I was getting for my £25. After staring at me a moment, obviously wondering how anyone had let me in at Dover or at Heathrow, she took pity and gave me the cogent answer: "Why, this booklet, of course." Even if I had thought of a response, she was already beckoning to the next dumb alien. Lamb's Conduit took on a whole new meaning.

The shorn lamb who wishes to stay beyond his allotted time gets to meet other representatives of Her Majesty's Government. Still naive, I assumed that my request to extend my one year visa by another two weeks would be handled as a mere formality. "I'd like to stay another fortnight." "Fine, Sir. Glad to have you. Cheerio."

The reality was not quite like that.

First of all, you have to telephone a branch of the Home Office. It took me most of an afternoon before anyone answered the phone. (In the United States they would have answered immediately and then put me on hold for the rest of the afternoon; so depending on whether you prefer canned music or the ringing pips on the telephone, it's pretty much the same. Of course, if you were put on hold in Britain, you would have to feed coins into the telephone box every few minutes while you waited.) I finally got through to a bored and somewhat curt gentleman who was not at all sanguine about my request.

"I'm a visitor," I said, "and would like to stay another two weeks."

"We do not normally permit such extensions, sir."

"But I have not yet finished my work," I said plaintively.

"What work, sir? I thought you were a visitor."

I figured I was getting into more and more trouble, but I went on: "I'm doing research at the University of London and the British Museum."

"Ah," he said in a completely changed tone. "Then, you are not a visitor. You are a Visiting Academic. That's rather different." I could hear the capital letters in VISITING ACADEMIC, and I knew how I would describe my status from now on. The magic words had entirely altered our relationship. He explained what I needed to do in order to turn the wheels of British bureaucracy. I would have to come down to Croydon, a southern suburb, within two months of my required departure date, bringing with me a bank statement to demonstrate that I would not be a burden to the British taxpayer, a note from the Institute of Historical Research, where I was working, to support my "need" to stay another fortnight, an optional letter from my department chairman at my home university indicating the date I would have to be back in the States, and an airplane ticket for the date I wanted to leave.

Overconfident at our new rapport, I pointed out to the Home Office spokesman the problems created by purchasing an airplane ticket for a date two weeks beyond my current visa permission. "Catch-22," I said.

"How's that, sir?"

"Catch-22. To get permission to leave on August 15, I have to buy a ticket for August 15 to show to you. But if you turn me down, then the ticket is no good to me. Catch-22."

There was a silence over the line. Then a little chuckle. "Quite right, sir. I see what you mean. A bit of a joke, is it?"

I thanked him, said I'd be in Croydon with the required documents in plenty of time, and yet once more vowed to myself to leave off joking.

I spent a long afternoon mingling with other assorted aliens at Croydon, but my status as VISITING ACADEMIC, my documents, and my airplane ticket simplified the process. (The chairman of my department at home got a little carried away when I requested a note: he *demanded* that I be back in Lawrence before the start of classes.) Two rubber stamps and I was back on the streets, so to speak.

Although I could stay until August 15, my automobile had to leave before the first of August. To avoid paying a Value Added Tax of 15 percent and a Motor Tax of 10 percent, we aliens must promise to export a car within one year from the date we bring it in. And there are no exceptions. You get a little white slip when you come through British Customs with your automobile, and you must produce this flimsy document on demand, a fact I did not quite register at the time.

On my first sabbatical Her Majesty's Customs Officer at Dover was a pleasant chap, a bit of a wag. As he waved our left-hand drive, German car through, he said, "You know we drive on the left in this country, don't you?" I assured him I knew that. "Tell you what, governor," he continued in a patter obviously being used not for the first time, "you just follow the car ahead of you when you leave here." Pause. "And hope it isn't another Yank." He, or his son, was still giving the same advice fourteen years later when I came through Dover with another German import.

Because some of us aliens are not as honest as others and do not ship our automobiles out of the country within a year, British Bobbies are encouraged to look for cars with telltale oval international registration plates and interrogate their drivers. During my last sabbatical I was stopped four times in London and began to understand how a ghetto youth might feel about repeated friendly attentions from zealous police officers.

The first time was the most alarming. Driving home late one afternoon from the British Museum, heading north on Tottenham Court Road, a four-lane, one-way street, I could see police officers out in the middle of the road, men in uniform as well as a few in suits and trenchcoats. They were pulling over an occasional car, and I, secure as always in my innocence, assumed a safety check (they do that sometimes), a sale of tickets for the Constables' Ball—anything but a dragnet for us registered aliens with our untaxed motor cars. I could not believe it when all the right-hand drive automobiles made it safely past the officers, and I—*I*—was directed to pull into an area in the middle of Tottenham Court Road.

A gentleman in plain clothes came over to my automobile, showed me some kind of identification, and motioned for me to roll down my window. I immediately forgot all the operating instructions on my fancy German car and could not lower the power window for him. Flustered, I found a button which immediately operated the rear window on the passenger's side. The officer shrugged and went around to the other side where he stuck his head through the rear window.

I asked to see his identification again—if in doubt, attack—and I now realized that he belonged to Her Majesty's Customs Office. He wanted to know if I had papers for the car. I had. They were locked in the glove compartment. In another three or four minutes I had figured out how to open the glove compartment and handed him my automobile registration documents. He leafed through the papers and asked to see my entry documentation. I gazed blankly at him.

"A small white sheet of paper? Stamped with your date of entry?"

I hadn't the foggiest idea.

"Where did you enter the country, sir?"

"Dover."

"And did they give you such a document, sir?"

I appreciated the patience and the politeness, but I could not recall anything about my 4:30 A.M. arrival after four hours on the night ferry from Ostende. I showed the officer my passport with the entry date for my body. It wasn't good enough. He wanted a white sheet of paper. While proper British drivers passed on either side, shaking their heads in disapproval at the illegal alien apprehended in the middle of Tottenham Court Road, the customs officer and I looked together through all the items which had accumulated in the glove compartment. A map of Dover. A pamphlet on the Amsterdam Zoo. A parking ticket from Brussels. (I don't think this item gained me any credit.) A postcard showing victorious Wellington at Waterloo. (Moderately helpful.) But no white entry paper.

Just as he was going to suggest the next step in the process for dealing with smugglers, I shook the map of Dover, which I had been holding—it wasn't an intentional shake: trembling is simply my usual method for dealing with authority—and out fell a white piece of paper. I handed it to him.

"That's it, sir," he smiled. "There all the time, was it?"

I was sent off with a cheery wave and the injunction to keep it "in a safe place." I pressed a button to roll my window up, and the AM-FM stereo radio went on. I eased back into the flow of traffic on Tottenham Court Road with a punk rock group blasting out through the open rear window.

The Customs Officer shook his head for a minute. Then he went back to pulling over those foreign cars with their odd plates and matching drivers.

SIXTEEN MINUTES TO
THE BRITISH MUSEUM

C onsidering the fact that I normally live 7,000 miles from the
British Museum, it may seem odd that when I reach London
on sabbatical, I look for lodgings as close to the B.M.
as possible. But I have always assumed I could do better than the
Edgware location—the last stop on the Northern Line, thirty minutes out—we settled for in 1969. For that year, a family embarking
for Nigeria agreed to rent their three-bedroom, semi-detached
house, complete with a gardener who came around weekly and a
window cleaner who came whenever he was short of cash.

Edgware, however, was a long way from Piccadilly and from the
scholarly pleasures of Bloomsbury. It took me forever to get to the
British Museum each day, whether I drove or walked to the corner,
caught the bus to the Edgware station and took the train down
past Burnt Oak, Colindale, Hendon Central, Brent, Golders Green,
Hampstead, Belsize Park, Chalk Farm, Camden Town, Mornington
Crescent, Euston, Warren Street, Goodge Street, and off at Tottenham Court Road. From there I walked the two blocks to the British
Museum.

Despite all that time spent in traveling, it was a good year. Our
eldest daughter attended the Orange Hill Grammar School, the
second one the local middle school, and the two-year-old stayed
home. The neighbors were pleasant enough, but they were not
"outgoing" in that peculiarly American way. Until, that is, the
morning when our astronauts landed on the moon. I had stayed
up most of the night to watch the landing on British television—I
think touchdown was around 3 A.M. in Britain—and I was bleary-eyed the next day. But as I set off on the long trek to the B.M., one
of the neighbors, who had hardly nodded before, touched his
bowler and said cheerily, "Well done, Yank!" I thanked him without quite knowing what it was I was thanking him for. After that, a

number of the people who lived on our block stopped for a brief chat. The Eagle had landed—in Edgware.

On my next leave, a semester in 1977, I was alone and did not have to worry about finding a flat with extra living space or one close to the schools. I looked for something closer in. I found it in Swiss Cottage, very near to the action in central London: I could drive to the British Museum in twelve minutes, to Piccadilly Circus in fourteen, and, if I was not apprehended by a Customs Officer, to the Tower of London or the National Theatre in sixteen minutes. Compared to Edgware, I was now practically rooming in the portico of the B.M.

The Swiss Cottage flat was on the bottom floor of a ramshackle late Victorian house, two blocks from the Swiss Cottage station on what is now the Jubilee Line and not too far from the Belsize Park stop on the Northern Line. Despite its prime location, it did have a few drawbacks. First of all, advertising it as a "garden apartment" had been stretching it a bit. It was three feet below ground level, and I was occasionally troubled by running water, stray alleycats attempting entry, and passing winos who would bend over and greet me pleasantly while I tried to sleep.

It had a tiny kitchen and an even smaller lavatory—loo, I mean. All the equipment was in the loo, including a tub approximately three and a half feet long and two feet deep. I kept my knees very clean for my entire sojourn in Swiss Cottage: they were always right there under my chin as I sat in the tub. And there was never any problem if I forgot something, say the shampoo, before I wedged myself in for a bath. I could reach anything in the room from where I sat immersed. It was quite convenient in its own way.

The battered and scratched furniture had obviously been assembled from a series of jumble sales—the British equivalent of rummage or yard sales. There was even a decrepit but working 12-inch, black-and-white television set. In America, we simply plug our sets in and settle down to watch Dan Rather or Dynasty or the Kansas City Chiefs versus the Green Bay Packers. In Britain today, you go to your local post office, fill out a form, fork over £62.50 for a color set, £21 for a black and white, and receive in return a

television license with an official stamp on it. Then you and your set are legal. But woe unto the viewer caught watching an unlicensed set. Generally, the authorities depend upon the honesty of the British public, but, just in case, there are ways of finding out who has not visited his friendly local post office this year. Remember the sinister dark vans with the rotating antennae in all those World War II films? The Nazis were always trying to pinpoint the transmitter with which the brave resistance fighters were signaling London. Today the local unlicensed residents watch out for the Post Office Mobile Listening Van with the same wariness Paul Muni and his friends were on the lookout for Helmut Dantine or Erich von Stroheim in the Hollywood version of occupied Prague or Copenhagen.

So the British authorities know if you are watching the telly. And they know who has purchased the little slips of paper with the official stamps on them. Perhaps less attuned than the natives to these dangers, I was caught unawares one morning in my damp little garden flat. Because I was only going to be there five months, I could see no good reason to plunk down the full licence fee (there are no part-year compromises) for the small grainy screen in the corner.

A sharp rap on the door startled me.

There were two of them. I would have settled for a pair of missionaries, but this was worse. "Do you have a television set, sir?" one of them wanted to know. They are always courteous, but this does not mean that they will not have you thrown into the Tower with the two young princes.

As in so many crises in my life, I weighed all the consequences in a matter of seconds and came up with the usual not-quite-first-rate answer.

"Yes," I said, "but it doesn't work very well so I never watch it."

When I analyze this sort of typical response to dangerous questions, I realize that there is a formula which seems to work most of the time. I offer two answers: "Yes. But, no." The reason it succeeds, I suspect, is not that my interrogator is fooled or impressed by my honesty, but rather that he or she cannot believe that I think I am going to get away with such marshmallow twaddle. They almost always lecture me on my misdemeanors and make me promise never again to do whatever it is that offends. I always promise solemnly, and they let me off "this time."

It worked again with the television police, but I must admit that I scurried down to the post office that afternoon and handed over the full amount for my last five weeks in London. It was not quite the same, viewing the telly without that little thrill of the illicit, but I figured a generous donation was better than the Tower, the butt of Malmsey, or The Block.

On my most recent sabbatical I laid out the cash for a color television license almost immediately after sighting the white cliffs of Dover. Finding a flat took a bit longer, although I was once again a bachelor and did not have to consider schools or extra closet space.

Before leaving North America I had composed an advertisement to run in the *Hampstead and Highgate Express*, the weekly newspaper covering the area north and northwest of central London. So for two weeks in July the *Ham and High* (I know it sounds like a sandwich, but that's what *they* call it) ran my "Visiting Academic" advert. When I reached London, I took a room in a small hotel and went round to the newspaper offices to collect the responses. There were nine of them. Although some were clearly unsuitable, a few had possibilities—of various kinds.

One of the more interesting was obviously too cramped—"just one room, albeit very pretty and with many fitted cupboards (made by a boat person!)." The woman who was offering the "very lovable room" would be sharing the kitchen and bathroom facilities with me "although," she wrote, "I live and have my being in the large studio room above." I suppose I might have been able to squeeze into the small room, but I was not at all sure I could sleep comfortably knowing that my landlady had her "being" right above me. She might, I decided, be a medium, and the comings and goings would be too much.

The response which most intrigued me came from a woman who had a "well-furnished" apartment in St. John's Wood, even closer in than my Swiss Cottage flat. What I did not understand was her line about the flat being "either £95 or £70" How could it be one or the other? I telephoned and asked. Despite a couple of attempts, I was unable to extract an explanation over the telephone. "Come see it," she said, "and I'll tell you." It was only a short drive from where I was staying, and when I saw the attractive brick apartment building, I was favorably impressed. I took the lift to the fifth floor and found her apartment. The friendly, middle-aged woman who answered the doorbell showed me about. The rent, it turned out, would be £95 a week or £70 a week depending on whether or not she came with the apartment. Well-furnished indeed! And, unlike such offers on the American Plan, here it would be less expensive if she came with the flat. However, we did not hit it off that well, and I left her to work out some satisfactory arrangement with the next gentleman caller.

Another possibility was a handsome ground-floor flat sidling right up to Hampstead Heath. However, when I spotted the two padlocks and deadbolt lock on *each* window, I checked my enthusiasm. Apparently, highwaymen still roam the Heath. Another landlord was showing me about his cozy flat and mentioned casually that the British Rail track was "fairly close by." At almost the same moment the house began to shake and a frightening roar drowned out all speech as the 3:14 went by. I suspect that at one time the back window was used to hang out the mail sacks which were hooked by the train as it thundered past a few inches away. "People get used to it," the landlord assured me as I hurried down the front steps. "After a few weeks," he shouted after me, "you won't even hear it."

The flat I finally chose was somewhat further out—in Golders Green. But it was peaceful, those who had their "beings" above me kept quiet about it, and I did not have to accommodate a friendly landlady. Most important, it met my primary requirement. Although Golders Green was a couple of miles past Swiss Cottage, on a good day, making all the lights and avoiding the slow lanes and traffic jams, I could whip my willing automobile down Finchley Road, around Regents Park, past the Post Office Tower, and up to the British Museum in sixteen minutes.

Without a tail wind, of course, it took longer.

ENDNOTE

SEPTEMBER SONG

Back in the sixties when I was a shiny assistant professor, getting ready for the academic year meant reading a few new books, skimming some old ones, sharpening lecture notes, and setting up the library reserve list. I was surprised to discover that to these activities my Kansas colleagues had added another: following closely the harvesting of the hard red winter-wheat crop. Even when they explained to me the connection between the wheat crop and faculty salaries, I could manage only a tolerant smile. Had I spent four years in graduate school to contemplate grain?

Reminiscing about those bucolic days, I am struck by the realization that early September would have been merely a pleasant twitch on the tail-end of summer then. Oh, a few eager freshmen might have been on their way to Ann Arbor or Ithaca, but seasoned professors would still have been lounging in the sun, junketing on the Continent, or puttering away happily in laboratories or libraries. They would have been *about* to consider gearing up for another academic year. But today, after twenty years of progress in education, by Labor Day my colleagues and I have been *teaching* for more than a week! How this came about, none of us knows. In place of the divinely ordered calendar of the past—no football games until mid-September, no classes until the third week— somebody, a few years back, persuaded us to start classes in August. Have you ever *been* in Kansas in August? Even the wheat has had the good sense to get itself harvested by the fourth of July. They assured us, these smooth-tongued academic snake-oil salesmen, that this schedule would be more efficient, that we would have more time between semesters in January. I keep looking for all those extra days we have saved just as I keep looking for all the money I have saved since 1962 when I gave up cigarettes or the extra cash which has been accumulating since my wife began to cut my hair in 1970.

During these abbreviated summers, I still revise my old notes and read a few books, but I also scrutinize the fine print in my professional liability policy in preparation for teaching in the Age of Litigation. It was not always thus. I can remember a conversation early in my career about liability insurance for faculty members.

"Give me an example," I asked the university attorney one sociable evening, "of the sorts of liabilities a professor might have."

He puffed thoughtfully at his cigar for a while before he offered an opinion: if a tall bookcase in my office were to topple onto a student, I might be sued. This example was sufficient for me to postpone getting coverage for another eight years. I did, however, stop buying heavy books.

Today's returning professor faces other new anxieties. According to recent newspaper accounts, a conservative organization is planting older students in classrooms to monitor the remarks of liberal teachers. Although I doubt that many literature professors will be under observation, I am vetting my lecture notes to be sure I do not present an inviting target. Figuratively speaking, that is. In other words, no more urging clemency for Richard III or questioning the right of Francis Macomber's wife to carry a rifle.

I have already had a taste of what it might be like. Not long ago I taught a course in "Persuasion." What *I* had in mind was a straightforward approach to writing effective prose. One of my more conservative students, however, envisioned a much more specialized course of study.

"I want to learn," he said, "how to persuade those pointy-headed liberals that they had better shape up." Smoothing the hair over the top of my head, I tried to interest him in the pleasures of paragraphing and topic sentences. After a few weeks he dropped the course—probably to join a more militant prose group. (Active Voice! No Modifiers!)

But liability insurance and classroom observers are individual worries: "student-athletes" are a new institutional concern.

Throughout the semester my vice-chancellor will be inviting me to "help the University monitor the progress of our student-athletes towards their degrees." On a variety of forms, I shall be expected to report the swimmer who has skipped her last three classes, the tight end who flunked the mid-term, and the half-miler who got out of the starting blocks a week early for Thanksgiving vacation.

Perhaps we had more responsible athletes in the olden days. I can still recall vividly the afternoon three weeks into the spring semester when a student from my Major British Writers class (Chaucer, Spenser, and Their Ilk) intercepted me on the steps outside the building.

"Professor Gold," he said, "I wanted to let you know that I won't be in class today. Or for the rest of the year. I just signed with the pros."

"Thank you, Mr. Sayers," I answered respectfully. "I appreciate your telling me." We shook hands, and he went off to the Chicago Bears for $200,000. Now *that's* what I call a student-athlete. (And he returned to complete his degree too.)

The legendary halfback has long since retired, but I am still here, scrambling to avoid the rush and survive the challenges of computerized enrollments and PCs in every dorm. My students no longer explain their late papers with "My grandmother was ill." Now it's "My floppy disk was erased," or "The ink-jet printer is down." I cannot imagine that shiny assistant professor of years ago writing into *his* syllabus: "No dot-matrix term papers." But Mr. Chips learns to change with the times. Besides, his eyesight is failing.

One of the more surprising changes is how closely these days I watch the Kansas wheat crop. You would not believe how anxiously someone raised on the south shore of Long Island can attend to the health and harvesting of winter wheat. But really! Have you seen those prices? Surely a nation which has landed a man on the moon could do better by its university professors than $2.90 a bushel!

How can any professor teach effectively at those prices?